F MY DAD

F

MY DAD

Overcoming the Anger, Rage, and Pain of being Fatherless

Q. Moore

Q. Moore

Published in St.Louis, Missouri
Publishing: Q.O. Moore LLC

Scripture quotations noted (ESV) The Holy Bible English Standard Version, Student Study Bible, Crossway Books (2011).
Scripture quotations noted The Message (MSG) are from Eugene H. Peterson and Mark A. Tabb, *The Message Remix*. Colorado Springs: Alive Communications, Inc, 2003.
Ice Cube. "Amerikkka's Most Wanted." 1990.
"The Incredible Hulk," Universal Television. 1977.
Merriam-Webster.com
Bing.Big.gov
Hopkinsmedicine.org
Strivemental.com
Worldpopulationreview.com
Digital Art of Trees, provided by Matt Gerling

ISBN:
ISBN: 979-8-9893793-0-9 (Paperback)
ISBN: 979-8-9893793-1-6 (eBook)

Dedication

This book is dedicated to my wife and children,
Sherri, Jasmine, Brittany, Tristen, and Skylar.
As well as my grandparents, my mama, and those who
were and still are a part of the village that raised and influenced
this boy into a man—you know who you are.

This is also dedicated to those who have battled the epidemic of fatherlessness.
I just want you to know that you can get the freedom your heart desires and
accept the fact that none of it was your fault.

Finally, I must dedicate this to God, my Heavenly Father, who has always been there even when I had no clue that he was watching over me.

Contents

About the Author (Rear Cover)

Q. Moore is a follower and believer in Jesus Christ, who is also a speaker with a God-given gift to connect and relate with any audience, whether large or small as well as young, old, and all ages in between. Mr. Moore is able to dive deeply into the topic of fatherless as he too grew up without a relationship with his biological father.

Mr. Moore has earned both an M.Div. (Master of Divinity) from Liberty University as well as a Master of Business Administration. With the combination of this education background, he has been able to enter the business world with a unique insight on society, all while directly connecting it with his Christian faith.

Mr. Moore will tell you that the most important role and position he's ever held in life is one of a husband and a father. He prides himself on being a man of God who carries family in the depths of his heart. "I just want to do whatever I can to make my Heavenly Father proud."

Foreword

Writing a book about yourself cannot be easy. Going down memory lane, remembering things your mind has stuffed away. Pain. Anger. Love. Stories. So much is on the pages of this book.

I can tell you that behind and underneath all of the words, there are emotions and experiences, that have shaped, chipped away, motivated, and persuaded the author throughout his life. Living a life without acknowledgment (that you are his child) and acceptance (that he wants you in his life) from your father while the community compares you to him or talks to you about him, had to be excruciating. Where does the hurt go? How much anger is within you? What is that anger doing to you? What is that anger doing and saying to those that love you? Where does the resentment lie? Who carries the pain? How do the messages of you not being good enough land within your heart? Who are you? Why are you here? Why doesn't he love you? Why doesn't he want you? How do you live with rejection? How do you love? So many questions that people don't always have the answers to.

Please allow this book to be your guide on how to connect to the One that can lead you through all the hurt and the pain. Knowing the one who has the answers and knows the heart of every man, scripture confirms that he will uphold, defend, sustain, administer justice to and through, preserve, deliver, and be a father to the fatherless. His Word is true, and He does and will continue to do everything that He has said. He is true to his word and faithful to perform it because He is not a man that he should lie. So, my prayer for anyone that reads this book or has experienced earthly fatherlessness is, "Lord, thank you for the people that read this book, and especially those who need you. Thank you for always defending, upholding and sustaining them. Thank you for always providing a way of escape as many are tempted to hold on to anger, resentment, and shame because of abandonment and rejection. Please heal the hearts of your children and cause those that do not know you to gain a desire to get to know you and open their troubled hearts to you. Amen" For the fathers who have not fathered their children well, "Lord, love them into a desire to repent, love you, and love their children. Amen."

Sherri M. Moore, MA, LPC.

Preface

When you picked up this book, I know what popped into your mind as you read the title. The profane F word is not written anywhere on the cover, it's written on the inside of you. Author George Eliot coined the phrase "Never judge a book by its cover." Well, I'd be lying if I didn't say that I carried that very sentiment in my heart toward my dad for nearly thirty years, and then something amazing happened—the profane "F" word became the word "Forgive." I needed to forgive my dad.

Fatherlessness is an epidemic that has been going on since the beginning of time. Many of the struggles that children, adolescents, and adults face, from anger to depression, may be linked directly to fatherlessness. Growing up without a father, I am able to directly connect with those who have personal struggles stemming from the lack of a relationship with their biological father. The ability to empathize with these readers, along with those who may have had healthy relationships with their fathers, is something I take to heart, a push from God to connect with those who have walked in my shoes.

The goal of this book is to help those who struggle with fatherlessness understand that their pain is real and that it wasn't their fault. The guidance in these pages will encourage the reader to embrace the lack of that relationship and know that it doesn't have to define their future for one more second, as it's the father that is missing out on them, not the other way around.

Every person wants to be accepted, approved, affirmed, and more than anything acknowledged by their father. But if that never happens, they can learn to grow and love themselves despite the absence of that paternal figure. In the end, the hope is to help the reader understand that their Heavenly Father has been there all along. As Jeremiah 1:5 says, "Before I formed you in the womb, I knew you."[1] This book will help you see the need for a relationship with Jesus Christ, as He says in John 14:6, "I am the way, and the truth, and the life. No one comes to the Father except through me." Jesus will be your guide to directly connect you to our Heavenly Father, as he already knows everything about you but would now like for you to know a little more about Him.

---

[1] Unless otherwise noted, all biblical passages referenced are in the ESV Student Study Bible, Crossway Books (2011).

Chapter One

Where's My Dad?

Around the age of five, I noticed all the pictures of my mother and me. As I started my first day of kindergarten, the school was an old house that was being used for kindergarten only. I noticed that some of the kids, who didn't look like me in color, were being dropped off with a mother and a father. I can't remember one father of color that was there with the mother and their child, including my own. It was very confusing, and I wondered why I didn't see any dads that were the same color as me. However, I was only five, and I knew a bunch of men who looked like me. There was my grandfather, my uncles, and men in the neighborhood, so I knew they existed. I understood that my grandfather was my mother's father, and he was married to my grandmother. They lived in the same house and had many children and grandchildren, a large family. My uncles had children, but it never really made sense to me.

My cousin Scott and I were like brothers, and we still are. He was two years older than me, and I spent a lot of time at their house with his two siblings, my cousins Junie and Christie. I can remember one day we were sitting down to eat dinner, and while we blessed the food, I looked around and it dawned on me again that my uncle was my cousin's dad. In that moment, I can remember thinking, *why don't I have a dad?*

My uncle Richard was strict, and he and my aunt Billie Sue ran a tight ship. I can remember my cousins having days mapped out as to who was doing what chores, and they also had a TV schedule as to which one of the three kids had a turn; this was what a family looked like to me. Everything else was a lot like my house, but the biggest difference were the siblings and the man of the house. Unc carried a certain presence about him. I mean, you knew he was in charge and so did all his children. My auntie carried a presence about her, too, as she was no joke either.

Strangely enough, I just enjoyed the thought of having siblings and there was a level of security knowing that my uncle was there that I can't really explain.

They had a family portrait, and I can remember just looking at it and seeing how it was so different than all the pictures at my house. I recall thinking, *Where is my dad?*

For every child that grows up fatherless, there always comes a time where the unknown meets reality. When you're an infant or a toddler, most people don't really have recollections of memories from those time-frames. However, it's amazing how far the mind can go back when trauma is involved. The moment I understood that I had a dad but he wasn't with us, the question that I always asked myself was, *Where is he?*

Most fatherless children won't pester their single parents about their fathers, and the ones that do usually get a spiel about how terrible a person he was and how he didn't want them anyway. I don't believe those responses are said to simply hurt the child, but they come from a place of pain, disappointment in themselves, and how difficult life is as a single mother. However, there are many single parents who never utter a bad word about the missing parent, and for those people who make that choice, I commend them. Let me say that I never heard my mother say anything bad about my father, for as long as I can remember.

The ultimate reason for their only being two people in the photo instead of three is that the single mother took on the responsibility to have a family, even if it meant only the two of them. The love for the one she carried would bond them forever, and if she loved hard enough, it would wipe away what was missing. Unfortunately, no matter how much love the single mother provided, it would never stop the longing for a man the child never knew.

For all of you single mothers out there, it is a spiritual connection to the divine order that God always intended, and you have no way of wiping that out. I commend all the single mothers who did their best to raise children on their own. I truly believe that one day, the Heavenly Father will say to you, "Well done." I also need to recognize the single fathers out there, as they do exist, and for all of them, you have my utmost respect. Children who were raised by single fathers with missing mothers is a whole other book.

Once a child understands that they have a father, and as they gaze into photos, noticing that someone is missing, immediately, without their understanding, the question of their identity enters their psyche. Questions like, "Do I look or act like him?" "Why did he leave us?" "Did my mom do something?" "Did I do something?" These are questions that in many situations may go unanswered forever. When they go unanswered, it can lead to looking for approval from people who aren't their fathers. For girls, maybe they look for what they should've received from their father in a young boy or even a young man. For boys, maybe they veer toward a group of other young men who suffer from the same fatherless condition. This may typically start with mischievous behavior and can often lead to far worse scenarios in life. The common denominator here is children who have identity issues that are directly connected to fatherlessness.

In the end, as it pertains to seeing only two instead of three in a family photo, it is a simple reality for so many children and so many adults who have experienced what it's like to simply wonder about the other half of themselves. It's a feeling that never truly goes away until you are introduced to your Heavenly Father, and then you'll have the opportunity to see and receive who you really are in His eyes and how much He truly loves you and all that He has in store for you.

As I go back and look at some of those photos now, as a grown man, I see a young mother who did her best to raise a man. However, when I look deeper at those pictures, I am reminded how my Heavenly Father was there all along, through the good, bad, and ugly times, but there were also some magnificent times that I am so grateful to have experienced.

It is easy for all of us to wallow in our hurt and our pain, and how many of those old pictures are painful reminders of what wasn't and who was missing, but if we would flip the script, if we've lived long enough to properly reflect, the fact that you have the ability to look back and remember is the gift and the proof that your Heavenly Father was there all along. Think of all the times that were absolutely magical; pause and be grateful.

Thanks, Mama, for choosing to have me.

The young lady calls her boyfriend. "Hello?"

"Hey... What's up?" he says.

"I'm pregnant," she replies.

He responds, "WHAT? Well, I'm not ready to be a father, so what are you going to do about it?"

God gives us all the free will to choose. We often use the word mistake instead of the correct word, which is either choice or decision. As it pertains to fatherlessness, it's not a mistake, because you were not a mistake. It doesn't matter if the man didn't mean to get the woman pregnant, there was a choice that was made to engage in sex, all the while knowing the possible consequences of that choice. So, if that choice was made to have sex in the heat of the moment, then how could the child be a mistake? Typically, the response goes something like, "I'm just not ready to be a father." However, you were more than ready to have sex, and again, you knew there was a chance that your decision could lead to fatherhood. When you aren't prepared to be a parent, the thought of getting someone pregnant, as a male, is constantly weighing on one's mind. However, that thought usually doesn't stop the yearning that seems to go from the top of the head to the bottom of one's feet. It's something that feels it just must be done, no matter the consequences. Now, in the heat of the moment, you throw caution and all reason out the window and get right down to it until the moment of ejaculation for a male. Most males, if they are careless and choose (there's that word again) to have unprotected sex, the thought immediately arises that, "I shouldn't have done that," or "I hope she was on the pill," even the classic line of, "I know I pulled out in time." Again, you had a choice. You had a choice to abstain from having sex at all, or you could've used protection, which we all know by now is not fail-proof, but either way—you had a choice.

As time passes and the male hears those words, "I'm late," it changes the trajectory of their lives forever. At that very moment, for those who know they will not stick around to be a father, for whatever the circumstance may be, there are many lines out there that have been used; "You trapped me,"

"I told you that I wasn't ready to be a father," "You need to get an abortion," "Having a baby will mess up my life," "How do I know it's mine," "I used a condom, so it can't be mine," "I know that you've been with other people," and the list goes on and on. The truth of the matter is that fear becomes the overwhelming emotion amongst both males and females, and this scenario is typically outside of being married.

At the time that the male chooses to give those responses, it still doesn't eliminate the choice that was made to have sex to begin with, and the one who gets lost in all of it is the child that has been conceived. See, during that moment, the child had no choice. The male, which will soon be a father in nine of the fastest months ever, has another choice to make; to stay and carry out his responsibilities or leave that up to the mother and her family.

Ladies, when you meet that oh so fine-looking man who seems to have eyes for you or your curves, one of the first questions you should ask is, "How is your relationship with your dad?" The answer to that question may tell you everything you need to know. Now, that shouldn't sway you ladies to freely give yourselves to them, but it will shed some light of what sort of man they may just turn out to be. These kinds of questions never come up, right? Especially not in the heat of the moment. However, maybe it should, as I believe that would probably cool things down quite a bit. Most men would probably respond with a big fat, "Huh?"

Ladies, if a man gives you any of the reasons that were mentioned earlier as to why he can't be a father, most of the time the choice has already been made and that child will grow up without a relationship with their biological father.

A female may be in a relationship and fear that the male is pulling away and he just might leave, and she believes having his baby will make him stay. Again, this is a "choice." The common theme in many of the bad choices or decisions we make is usually because we are putting ourselves first in the most selfish way. We want what we want, when we want it, by any means necessary, even if it means destroying a life before it can ever speak for itself.

What if you did get married and you two were madly in love and couldn't wait to start a family, and when the mother gets to be about six months pregnant, the honeymoon phase is long gone and one or both parties see fit to call it quits before it ever really started, and divorce is the only result that seems to be the best "choice." The child has no say, he or she is not even born yet, yet the decision will be made.

Our society today will tell us that there are plenty of kids that survive divorce and everything comes out fine; however, statistics say otherwise, but that's another topic. We are strictly talking about men who choose to no longer or never be a father to the child who they played a major part in conceiving. God will never stop us from our free will to choose, but He will always care for and love on the ones who never had a choice, and those are the fatherless.

When my son was born, I sobbed like a baby, and I didn't really know why. I mean, it was uncontrollable. My poor, sweet wife was trying to console me after hours and hours of labor and pain. She stroked my head, asking, "What's wrong?" I can remember looking up at her and saying, "How could someone ever choose to leave?" At that moment, I knew that it would take death to keep me out of the life of my children, and that was the choice that I made right then and there.

My son came into this earth face up, which is known as OP or Occiput Posterior position. He couldn't breathe through much of the delivery, and his lips were blue when he arrived, but then he belted out a cry, and I knew he came out face up just to make sure that the first face he saw was his father and to make sure that I would be there. As a matter of fact, I pulled him out from my wife's womb, and thus my choice to be a father was solidified, and I knew that I would never leave like my father chose to leave me.

Before it was a popular reality TV show, it was my life. My mother became pregnant with me at the age of seventeen. This was in the mid-1970s. Now, just think of this, the number one R&B song in 1973 was "Let's Get It On" by Marvin Gaye, need I say more? Two teenage kids, listening to the smooth sounds of an R&B legend, and the topic being about sex—I mean, I can't make this stuff up.

In the end, their decision to have sex led to me. Do you think that they thought about their lives together as a loving family, or do you think that my mother was happy that some young popular guy was interested in her, and my father was just looking to get some? Let's keep it real, I don't have time to sugarcoat anything, as lives are at stake. So many lives have been damaged because of the choices made by individuals who simply weren't ready to become parents, especially teenage parents.

See, God created a certain protocol or hierarchy, which is boy becomes man, man becomes husband, husband becomes father. Girl becomes woman, woman becomes wife, wife becomes mother. As we all know, there are plenty of situations, like my own, where boy and girl become parents, bypassing both adulthood and marriage, and whether they are ready or not, a child was conceived, and most of the time so was dysfunction.

There was a hip-hop song back in the 80s from a rapper named Slick Rick titled "A Teenage Love," and a part of the hook was "...don't hurt me again." If you haven't been able to tell by now from reading this book, the author is what you would call a music-head. The reason that I brought up "Let's Get It On" and "A Teenage Love" is that I would like to touch on the influential power of music and how this stuff is deeply spiritual. Most people have heard of the devil, also known as Satan, Lucifer, or Beelzebub. However, did you know that Lucifer was the angel of music before he was cast out of heaven? If you don't believe me, research it for yourself. The thing with that is though he was cast out of heaven, he didn't lose his musical gift, and he is the master of deception, and music can be an amazing influential tool.

Now, I'm not hating on music; again, I'm a music-head, but I'd be wrong if I didn't admit the power of musical influence, especially as it pertains to teenagers and sex. Life as a teen revolves around music. Think of some of your favorite songs as a teen and then question the lyrical content. If you're being honest with yourself, it'll be easy to see how the lyrics are used to influence people, and my mama was and is a lover of all kinds of music.

Though the music, lyrics, and beats, didn't make anyone do anything, there is no denying the power of its influence.

In John 10:10, Jesus describes Satan as the following, *"The thief comes only to steal and kill and destroy. I came that they may have life and have it abundantly."*[2] The thing that stands out here is that Satan is described as a thief. Do I have to break down what a thief does? They rob you of something, and more times than not, it's

---

[2] Ibid.

something valuable. So, is musical influence the cause of the choices that people make? Ultimately, no, people are responsible for the choices they make, but we are kidding ourselves if we don't admit that there is influential power in music.

My teenage mama was the tenth of eleven children, coming from a home where she was raised by her mother and her biological father. They were God-fearing people but not perfect. Can you imagine being a part of a household that had eleven children? Some of you may be able to relate, but I can only imagine how nearly impossible it would be to give every child the amount of attention they deserve.

My mother and all her siblings had the utmost respect for their parents, and I know that they longed for gentleness, kindness, and loving hugs and kisses from their mother, but I believe it's safe to say they didn't always receive what they desired. I mean, let's be honest, many of us don't have much left to give with just one child, now imagine if you had eleven. The point that I'm trying to make is that I believe that my mother desperately needed the love, affection, and attention from her mother and didn't really receive it.

I truly believe that there are many young ladies who desired those things from their mothers but many of them desired that from their father as well. I love my mother, and I know that she was a child raising a child and that she battled with mental health issues for years. I didn't really know that back then, as it wasn't a topic people discussed like they do today. All I can remember is that the adults in my life would always tell me, "Your mama's sick." That meant that she would be away in a hospital for a while. Again, I can't imagine how hard it must've been to raise a child and you were a child. Though my mother and I have never discussed those days, I believe that getting pregnant with me broke something in her, not because of me but because of my father.

Like I stated earlier, she was my biggest fan and still comes in a close second to my wife today. The father is the one who provides a little girl with the security of who she is and to never settle for someone who doesn't love them as much as their daddy. However, if daddy is missing, they are more likely to seek out the first male figure who seems to show them love and adoration.

Daddy provides a sense of self-worth, and if a young girl is seeking that from a young boy, in which he himself grew up without the proper relationship with his father, that usually doesn't equal happily ever after. Again, all of that creates a generational cycle of dysfunction, and the child has no say in the environment in which they are born into.

Mama was my biggest fan, and from her, I received love and affection, but she was not ready, neither mentally nor emotionally, to be a mother at the age of seventeen. In all honesty, what teenage mom is really ready to parent a child?

As for my dad, I can't say that I really know too much other than what I was told throughout the neighborhood. All I ever heard was that he was a good basketball player. I have played every scenario over in my mind, and the one that just doesn't stick is that they were madly in love and thought they were going to be together forever. Maybe my mother did, but I'm quite certain that my father didn't. I'm sure that my mother was just another piece of... well, I'll let you fill in the blanks. Look, the only way that I can write this is to keep it as real as I possibly can and that's it.

I believe that my father would fit the stereotypical star high school athlete, which will usually carry an arrogance, cockiness, a conceitedness that grows every time someone cheers their name, or every time people gloat over them and tell them how great and wonderful they are, even if it's simply for the way they can play a sport. I can only imagine how my mother felt when she found out that my father "liked" her. I mean, the star player liked her, wow. In my mind, on the outside looking in, he saw her as an innocent target for sex. Now, let's be clear, I'm not sure how innocent she was, but at the age of seventeen, living under her God-fearing parents, freedom was not something that the teenage daughters of the Moore household received easily, and with the lack of attention that I mentioned earlier, in a house with eleven children, she was open to the idea of being loved by a young man. Out of all the girls in school, he chose her.

Here's where I've thought of every possible scenario of how things went down. I mean, where I was conceived has never been discussed, but what if it was in the back seat of a car, hormones raging out of control with no other place available to do what they both desired to do. Maybe my father threw the lines on her that most promiscuous teenage males use in the heat of the moment. "I thought you loved me," "If you loved me you would want to do it too," "I didn't know you were a little girl," "I love you so much," "You're all I think about," "Let me just put it in and then I'll take it out." Maybe, ladies, you've never heard these lines before, and, men, maybe you've never used any of these lines before, and if so, consider yourself blessed. However, for many readers, they will know all about those lines, and either way, most of the time, the female is either influenced or pressured by the male. Now, let me be quite clear, there are more than enough teenage females out there who are ready, willing, and desiring the same thing as the male, and I believe that point must be mentioned. In the cases of those teenage girls, the question must be asked; what was the relationship like with their biological father, and whether they may have experienced some sort of sexual trauma as a child?

Back to my parents, the thought of what could happen may have loomed, the thought of pregnancy, what their parents would do to them, how would they be able to take care of a child, and in a matter of minutes, lives would change forever. In the end, I was conceived. As soon as ejaculation took place, I'm sure the fear was overwhelming. The young man zips up, and I can only assume that if the young girl was in love, she may have felt special, but I can only imagine the fear that sex was the only thing the young man desired, nothing more, including the likes of her.

Either way, an egg had been fertilized, and thus the process of life began.

In many cases, the man loses interest in the girl and the girl deals with fear, guilt, shame, and condemnation while a child forms in her womb.

I have no idea if this is exactly how this was carried out or not, but again, I have created every possible scenario of how I was created because it played a major part in my identity issues for decades to come.

As it pertains to my father, though, he may have been an arrogant basketball star, but he was still a teenage boy. The question that often comes to mind for me is what was the relationship like with his own father? Were they close? Was his father a womanizer? You know, "Papa was a rollin' stone." Was his father abusive to his mother? Maybe my father was abused himself. I'm not saying that any of this is the case, but when you don't know and are born with a creative mind, you spend a lot of time trying to figure out where you come from in order to determine who you are and why your father chose a life without you, his first-born son.

Many may think that these kinds of thoughts and actions are only relevant in minority or poverty-stricken environments. But, no, these sorts of thoughts and actions are prevalent all over the world and have been since the beginning of time.

Think about when sin took place in the beginning. Adam and Eve were deceived, influenced by a spirit that was opposite of God. Do you understand how powerful that influence had to be for two people who had direct access to God Himself? So, why is it so hard to believe that anyone could be influenced by this same dark spirit that we know as Satan? The thing is, he can only influence; mankind will always have a right to choose.

The Apostle Paul teaches in 1ˢᵗ Corinthians 10:13, *'No temptation has overtaken you that is not common to man. God is faithful, and he will not let you be tempted beyond your ability, but with the temptation he will also provide the way of escape, that you may be able to endure it."*[3]

Maybe you've been in some of the scenarios that I've described and gave in to the temptation; don't worry, we all have.

As Romans 3:23 says, *"...for all have sinned and fall short of the glory of God."*[4]

Maybe you were conceived by one of the scenarios given, or even worse than I described. That doesn't matter though, because you are not a mistake.

Always remember Jeremiah 1:5, *"Before I formed you in the womb, I knew you..."*[5]

So, you see, I had to be created in this way in order to be here during this particular time to reach you, right where you are, so that

---

[3] Ibid.
[4] Ibid.
[5] Ibid.

I could tell you that God knew you before you were ever conceived.

I believe that you, too, have a story to tell that could be influential to someone; we all do, and if you have struggled with being fatherless, please know that you're not alone, you've never been alone, scripture confirms it.

Chapter Two
The Village

If you're from where I'm from, then you would be familiar with the Projects, the East Bottom, and the New Addition (not to be confused with New Edition the music group). These were the neighborhoods that typically housed minorities. Notice that I didn't say that everyone was poverty-stricken in these areas, as there were many hard-working people who held down jobs in order to provide for their families. I truly believe that these kinds of neighborhoods, or "Hoods," exist in nearly every city or town on the planet. When you create environments for minorities, there's no doubt that the door is open for lower-income living, which can often lead to poverty-stricken mentalities. These are mentalities that can only see life through the scope in which they currently live or have lived. This mentality is not always limited to being a minority, as there are plenty of low-income majority neighborhoods as well. The reason for pointing this out is to once again shed light on the absence of fathers.

Don't get me wrong, though many fathers may have been absent in my environment, there were and are so many strong mothers and women that I could mention here that it might just end the chapter. Though these mothers may be incredibly strong, they were never supposed to raise children alone, as they didn't make them alone. I've heard so many mothers make the statement, "I can't make him a man." This may be true, but I believe this statement is often made from the frustration of a man not taking care of his responsibility as a father and leaving the mother and her children alone to fend for themselves.

When I was growing up, most of us traveled either by foot or by bicycle to wherever we needed to go. Not very many single mothers had their own car; they relied on others to provide transportation, and in many cities, public transportation was the primary means of getting from place to place, mostly by bus or by train. The reason for laying this out is because single parenthood is an absolute struggle from the very moment that the father decides he no longer wants to be in the role for which he had been called from the time of conception.

Father, Daddy, Dad, or Pops, whichever one may be used, holds a sense of pride, but only when a man is truly carrying out the role.

See, the father should be the provider, the protector, the leader, the teacher, as well as the disciplinarian. The father should follow a particular set of standards that provide his children with the example of not only how a son should be a father in his time but also the example for a daughter in how a husband is supposed to treat his wife. However, when you come from a fatherless environment, you don't always see those examples from the father, you get them from grandpa, uncle, cousin, or people you look up to on the street, as those may be the only examples of an adult male that many fatherless children encounter on a regular basis. These men can provide love and insight, but there's always the question of the relationship or the lack thereof with their own fathers, and thus the cycle of fatherless views can be passed down from generation to generation. Though these individuals may be a part of a village, they were never designed to take the place of a father, and many of them are never married to the mother or mothers of their children.

Now that we have identified the role of the father, it's easy to see the struggle that a child can face from the very beginning. Many grow up in poverty-stricken conditions. They may need the aid of government assistance, as one income just isn't enough to supply the needs of raising a child, let alone multiple children.

When I was growing up, my mother received government assistance. You know what it's like to get a block of cheese and several blocks of butter along with powdered milk? You would use food stamps, which were paper coupons that was a similar tender like money but only for products that could be eaten. To this day, I carry one in my wallet, and every now and then I'll pull it out and glance at it. This is only to remember where I came from and how far my Heavenly Father has brought me, and it also serves as a reminder to always remain in a state of gratefulness.

Clothing may have to be obtained by means of hand-me-downs, thrift stores, garage/rummage sales, or if the mother or some other family member was a gifted seamstress. In the African American community that I grew up in, appearance was highly important. Knowing and learning how to do laundry, ironing your clothes, and how to use spray starch were a part of the norm. Even if you didn't have clothes that you wanted or were handed down by someone else, they needed to be clean and neat, as this was the standard. What sort of sneakers you wore were major and still is to this day. The worst sort of "joanin'," which basically means teasing, making fun of, or even bullying, would occur on a consistent basis based upon your appearance. If you didn't have name-brand sneakers, you were a target, and the nickname for those kinds of shoes were "buddies," "buster browns," "zips," and where I was from, they were called "dobbies." It was a brutal form of torment that a young person would face almost on a daily basis, even though they had no control of the kinds of shoes and clothing that their parents or parent could afford.

I can remember when we would anxiously await the government check. I always knew when the check would arrive, as that brown envelope would show up in the mail. Today, I'm certain that this is electronically done, and food stamps arrive on an EBT card., which stands for Electronic Benefit Transfer. I can remember how embarrassing it used to be having to shop with food stamps when I was a kid. We would look in the store to make sure we didn't see someone that we knew before entering. We would take a one-dollar food stamp and go into a store and buy a three-cent piece of gum to receive ninety-seven cents in return. We might hit up five different stores and do the same thing to have close to five dollars in change.

In all honesty, we didn't really know anything different, we were only trying to survive. Parents and especially single mother households felt the pressure to make sure that their children had nice clothes and name brand shoes. Typically, the overall goal was to provide the illusion that we weren't poor, and this kind of living is an element of a poverty-stricken mentality. Caring how you are viewed by others is in us all, it just depends to what degree.

The fact is that lower-income children may have to face these struggles on a daily basis, and what may follow is a barrage of teasing and bullying that in most cases will lead to some level of violence, mostly in self-defense. Deep down, fighting isn't only about protecting or standing up for oneself; for me, it was a fight against the one who was not only supposed to protect me or provide a better way of life but to also teach me how to protect myself.

When you are a product of this kind of environment, absent the love and wisdom of a father, the only thing that you know for certain is that the struggle is real and thank God for Mama. There is a lot to learn from the struggle. One may learn strength, survival skills, persistence, and the willingness to overcome. However, many may learn nothing other than what the world or the streets have to offer—drugs, alcohol, promiscuity, gambling, and so much more. It all sounds kind of fun, doesn't it? Well, maybe, until the consequences all come full circle, which typically ends in some fashion of death; physically, emotionally, mentally, or spiritually.

Maybe all of the above, as it's written in Romans 6:23, *"For the wages of sin is death, but the gift God is eternal life."*[6]

A verse that single mothers may teach, but fathers have been granted the ability to make it sink in through the stories of his own life.

If you grew up with both parents and have a loving family, consider it a true blessing. However, you may want to look at those around you and know that one out of every five may have a fatherless story. If you're anything like me and came from a similar environment, such as the one mentioned earlier in this chapter, hopefully the village in which you were raised was able to steer you onto the straight and narrow path.

Before you become quick to judge someone who may or may not look like you, has less than you, talks in broken English or

---

[6] Ibid.

maybe even a foreign language, quietly ask yourself if maybe they have or are currently experiencing some form of fatherlessness.

Though the negative percentages of fatherlessness are high, none of the percentages are one hundred percent, and those mothers, villagers, and overcomers deserve to be applauded. So, for that, I thank my village, you know who you are.

404 Rocheport Street is the address of a house in small-town America, but for me, it was a safe haven. Everyone has that place where they are or were the most comfortable; the place they can be themselves in their rawest and purest forms. Usually, this place is called home.

When I think back, my mother and I moved at least ten times that I can fully remember. As a kid, I didn't really pay much attention to it. For the most part, I stayed in the same school district, leaving the district twice, once in first grade and again a semester in sixth grade. The one thing that I always knew, no matter how many places we moved to, 404 Rocheport Street was home. It was the home of Bill and Sue, my grandparents, with whom I spent a lot of my years growing up there.

If I added the number of days that I spent in each location with my mother, it wouldn't come close to the amount of time that I spent at my grandparents. That residence would surely define the word family for me.

You may be asking "why?" Well, because there was a mother and father who were married, and, through my lens, were quite successful. Not successful as far as being wealthy but simply because they were a couple that was older yet still together. For the fatherless, that equals success.

Bill and Sue were known in this small community as good people. They were highly respected by everyone, black and white. In those days, being respected by white people truly meant something, but being respected by the black folks, well, that was a richness that is indescribable. They had eleven children, the ages ranging between the oldest and the youngest about twenty years apart. They had over a hundred grand and great-grandchildren combined and remained married for forty-four years. Remaining married for that length of time has a profound impact on many of the statistics that seem to be caused by fatherlessness. When the father is in his rightful place, there is a sense of security, safety, and knowing that no matter what, everything was going to be alright.

They were rather unique people, always willing to help someone in need, and both were believers in Jesus Christ. As the story goes, they would hold Sunday night Bible study, just for their immediate family. Everyone had to stay in on Sunday evenings, read, and discuss the Bible. Even if friends of other households had come over to visit and happened to be in the house on a Sunday night when Bible study was about to start, they were stuck and had to stay. These were the days when you'd literally see kids running home before the streetlight came on. The days when spankings or whippings (pronounced "Whoopins" where I'm from) was a form of punishment and correction. These two things are so different than using the word beatings, which many did receive, but that was far worse than a spanking.

Spanking is a direct instruction from God, as Proverbs 23:13-14 says, *"Do not withhold discipline from a child; If you strike him with the rod, he will not die."*[7]

Though this was the norm, in many of the black neighborhoods, if you acted up at someone else's house, they had the authority to

---

[7] Ibid.

spank you at their house and you would more than likely get another one when you got home. This was not some form of abuse but a form of correction that seemed to have a strong and often painful impact. When I think about the friends of my grandparents' children, my aunts and uncles, that would get stuck and have to stay for Bible study, I often wonder, how many of the friends that came over to that house wanted to come over during that time, because if they were fatherless, they were experiencing the power of the father's role in a way that only God could've intended.

Again, my grandparents were not perfect people, they went through many trials and tribulations in life, my grandmother's sister was murdered in her early thirties, leaving behind two children. Their house was destroyed by fire, and my grandmother had to pull my mother out, as a little girl, by her hair. If you are a loving mother, you will do anything to protect your children, and with the father in his proper role, he protects his wife and his children as well.

My grandfather was a smart man who had become blind in the late 1950s due to Glaucoma. He had an amazing wit and personality and the ability to tell stories that most anyone would be interested in listening to every word he had to say. He had a photographic memory, and though he was blind, all his other senses were extremely sharp.

One thing that I'll never forget my grandfather saying to me is, "Don't do anything to mess up the family name. We have a good name around here, and believe me, that was earned, so don't go and mess it up, because all you really have is your name that is directly attached to your character." I passed that same message on to my son, and maybe one day if he has a son, hopefully, it will be passed on to him.

I can remember my grandpa as a fun-loving person. He loved the St. Louis Cardinals baseball team and would whoop and holler during those games. I can remember him hollering during the 1982 World Series that the Cardinals won when I was eight years old. I would run in the room where he listened to the game, and he said, "They did it, Quinny, they did it, the Cardinals won!!!" He grabbed me and tickled me, as he often would, with those big, hard fingers. He would use those same fingers to bang on the door in order to wake me up for school. I was startled every morning.

He was easygoing, though, at least with me, and I would simply say on most Monday mornings, "I'm not feeling good today," and that was it. He would walk back to the kitchen and tell grandma that I wasn't going today. He would say, "Mama, he's not feeling good today." Later, in those afternoons, when he heard me playing around the house, he would always say, "Oh, you're going to school tomorrow."

I only had him for fourteen years, before he passed away. That was really the first time that I attended the funeral of someone I truly loved. I can remember how I felt during the repast, I couldn't understand why everyone was laughing, eating, and enjoying themselves right after putting him in the ground. I stepped away and simply walked around the town by myself and thought of the times with my grandfather and how I was going to miss him.

My Heavenly Father gave me my grandfather to allow me to see a man in his proper role of both a husband and a father. Thank you, Grandpa!

My grandparents ran a tight ship, and every one of us was raised to say "Yes, sir," and "No, ma'am." Not only to them but to any elder you may come across. It was standard across the board and throughout our community. That sort of thing has been lost in generations after mine, the respect for our elders has been diminished.

Grandma was also a mama bear, as I previously mentioned, who would stand, fight, and die for her children. My grandmother and I had a very close relationship, and that may be putting it lightly. I know that my grandmother loved all her children, grandchildren, and great-grandchildren, but my bond with her was really close. After a house full of children that were now adults, it was only me, and I believe she was able to enjoy parenting without all the stress.

I never questioned my mother's love for me, but my grandmother was like my hero. There are so many things that I say today that she would say. I could make her laugh hysterically. So much that she would begin to cough and say, "Quit, boy!!"

She was so protective of me. I used to have bad allergies, I still do, and my cousin Scott would have to cut my grandmother's grass with his dad. One day, it had to be a hundred degrees outside, and he was out there pushing a lawnmower. My grandmother would say, "Quinny can't be around freshly cut grass." So that day, as he was outside in that blazing sun, I stood in the kitchen window until I got his attention and was sipping on a soda. He was furious, but I was spoiled by my grandmother, my mother, and pretty much every adult in the village.

My mother probably spoiled me the most. I can remember almost always getting everything I wanted for Christmas and birthdays. When you're a kid, you have no real sense of money, you simply know who has and who doesn't. I knew my mother and I didn't have much, but she always did what she could to get what I wanted.

One particular spring, a store in town put a brand-new bike in the window that everybody wanted. Almost every day, we would walk past that store window and argue about who was going to get it. The truth of the matter was, I don't think any of us really believed that we had a chance to get that bike. It was one-hundred and forty-four dollars, as the tag that hung from the handlebars said. A couple months later, for my birthday, there it was, the Cobra bike. My mother had bought it for me. She always did things like that. I can remember being one of the first people in the neighborhood who had the original Nintendo. It came with Mario Bros and Duck Hunt. My bedroom would be packed with boys arguing for a chance to play. One year, on my birthday, my mother was responsible for one of the largest slumber parties ever. We lived in a run-down house that was owned by my grandmother, and my mom invited almost every kid in junior high, both white and black. Seeing a large group of white and black kids walking into a black neighborhood carrying blankets, sleeping bags, and pillows was unheard of, but my mama made it happen. Right or wrong, she always made it happen for me.

My grandmother would play tough for a while, and then she would eventually give in and give me almost whatever I asked for, but she always told me, "There are three things that I'll never do for my kids, buy them a car, buy them a gun, or bail them out of jail." She meant that, and so I never had to ask for any of those items.

I believe they all loved me dearly, but I also believe that they all felt sorry for me because of my having to grow up without a father. I mentioned how my grandmother was my hero, and to sum that up, one final story about her comes to mind. I was attending an elementary school in a different town from where my grandparents lived. My mother went into the hospital, and a teacher or principal came to get me out of class. "Grab your things, as you'll be leaving," she said. I grabbed my jacket and backpack, and then she said, "No, grab everything, as you will be leaving this school today." I had no idea what was going on and began to worry about my mom. Was she okay? Did something happen? I was probably around six years old at the time. When I stepped out into the hall, I could see my grandma at the end of the hallway. She was dressed like she was going to church. She had on a white suit with a white hat. I took off running down the long hallway, which felt like it was three miles to me, but I ran as hard as I could and hugged her around her waist, as I was so happy to see her.

She said, "C'mon, now, you're going home," and I always knew where home was for me, 404 Rocheport Street. Love you, Grandma, I miss you so very much, and thank you!!

Bill and Sue would be considered at the top of my village hierarchy, as there is so much of them in me as I strive to continue to make them proud. They were true heroes to many, but they were my definition of security and safety. Thank you, Grandma and Grandpa for everything, but more importantly, thank you for sticking it out and staying together. It turned out to be more valuable than you could've ever imagined.

The overall safety wasn't in the physical house, but what was inside that was priceless. See, God's protocol of boy becoming a man, man becoming a husband, and a husband becoming a father is the blueprint of a sustainable legacy that can last throughout future generations. Those of us who have struggled with fatherlessness on this earth are missing a piece of their identity, which in turn can have a major impact on the legacy that God always intended for us. If you were fatherless but can say you had a safe haven, count it as a true blessing, and for most of us it is the hub from where our village begins.

There's an old saying that goes, "It takes a village to raise a child." Though this could be seen as a biblical principle, it is not an actual verse of scripture in the Bible but comes from an African proverb. However, for many fatherless children, like me, it's absolutely true. I mentioned earlier that most people who grew up with their fathers being absent struggle with identity issues, not truly knowing who you are, as the history of one half of your bloodline is missing. For me, it was predominantly the Moore family, but there were so many other households involved, some black, some white, some brown. The village is simply the people in your life who provided some sort of insight, love, affection, and protection over you.

There was my mother, who was a young mom, still trying to figure out life herself. However, she always showed me love, affection, and a lifetime of encouragement. She was the fun mom, aunt, and sister, who had a heart to be there for anyone who may be in need. Today, she is a Pastor and is still pouring into the lives of people.

Previously, I spoke about my grandparents and how they were heads of the village. There were my cousins, many of them like siblings to me. I can't name them all, but they know who they are and the impact they've had on my life. Then there were my aunts and uncles, my stepfather, my pastors, my brothers, my friends, my teammates, and my coaches.

It's important that I mention the adults in this chapter who played significant roles in this village. The reason for this is not only to acknowledge them but to help you focus on the people who had some sort of positive impact on your life even though your biological father may have been missing in some way, shape, or form.

I've already mentioned my mother, who everyone called "Lesta," but she married a man named Jeff, who became my stepfather. I never called him Dad, but it wasn't personal, I just could never bring myself to say the word Dad. When I became an adult, I would always introduce them as my parents and say, "This is my mother and my father" out of respect, as he's earned it. I believe that Jeff and my mom began dating when I was about seven years old, though they didn't get married until ten years later. Jeff was a cool guy, who never really disciplined me or anything, the one thing that I learned from Jeff was how to detail a car. You have to take your time and the job is not complete unless the tires are wet (shining), the wheels sparkling and it must smell good, so, if you don't know, now you know. All I knew was that he worked hard and sacrificed thirty plus years at a plant to help support my mother and I as well as his son with my mother, my brother Derrick.

My brother Derrick and I are nine years apart, and he is a gifted singer and musician. We talk more now, as I believe life is bringing us closer together. I'm amazed by how he's a self-made musician on multiple instruments, and I know that it can be nothing less than a gift from God.

It was always hard for me with my mom, my stepdad, and my brother, as I often looked at them like that was their family. No offense meant to Jeff, but that wasn't my father. I never voiced anything like that, but that's how I felt. I'm sure my stepdaughters felt the same way about me as they got older.

Again, Jeff and I are cool, and one moment with him sticks out in my mind. I called home to tell them that my wife and I had just purchased our first home, and I heard Jeff scream in the background, "WHOO!!!" I had never heard him respond like that to anything that had pertained to me. I believe he was proud of me, as owning a home to black people really meant something. I didn't realize that before, but in that moment, I understood. Since I was so young when Jeff and my mom began dating, I was always around his family, and they always treated me like their own; shoot, we were family.

Jeff had a twin brother named Greg. Greg was always one of the nicest people I've ever met. If you were ever to have an encounter with Greg, you would immediately see the kindness that dwells in his heart immediately. An easy-going, gentle guy, who again, was extremely nice to me and it's something that I'll never forget.

I had a close relationship with my uncle and aunt, Gary and Elaine, and especially with their son Gordon, we were tight growing up. I remember my aunt Elaine being the lady in fourth grade who came to our school to do the nutrition test with rats. I'm sure some of y'all remember feeding one rat healthy food and the other one junk food and watching the rat that ate junk food get bigger and slower while the rat that ate the nutritious food stayed lean and active on the little wheel in his cage. I thought it was so cool that she was the lady doing that. There was a sense of pride there, as she was a smart and successful lady.

My Uncle Gary, Jeff's brother, was an ex-high school basketball legend like my Uncle L.D. I believe they actually played against one another. I would spend a few summer weekends with them during junior high and the first couple of years of high school. Gordon and I would play in basketball tournaments and whatnot.

As you can see, I was always attracted to homes where there was a husband and wife who had children together and saw fit to stay together.

Jeff's mom was a sweet lady, too. She loved sports. I was always amazed at how much she knew about basketball and even more amazed when she knew how I played. Mrs. Dolores would say, "I saw you had eighteen points last night, uh-huh."

I thank the whole family for treating me like family, especially my extended cousins, Gordon, Brian, Brent, Terrell, and Eddie. There are so many more, but I had to name those because I seemed to be around them the most. Believe me, they know who they are.

My oldest aunts and uncle, Nathaniel, Florence, and Sharlon, were all good people, they lived in different states, so I didn't see them very often. My aunt Florence lived in Kansas City with her four children, my cousins, Melvin Jr, Tasha, Anthony, and Joe. We saw them more often, and Melvin Jr. lived in the same town that I did.

One story that has to be told as it is directly connected to the village is when my cousin Joe came to live with his brother, Melvin Jr., and they stayed in the projects. I looked up to Joe, I always thought he was cool because he was a city kid. I'm not exactly sure what sparked this incident, but I had to be about fourteen or fifteen at the time. I was chillin' with Joe, and Melvin Jr., who always worked hard and kept a job, walked through the door. I could tell that he was surprised to see me there, more than he was surprised that Joe was just chillin', doing nothing. As Melvin Jr, walked into the apartment, he walked straight to his room and didn't say a word.

Seconds later, he rushed from the back room and tackled Joe on the couch, and a fight ensued. We would note these kind of incidents as "Furniture was moving up in that piece." Melvin Jr. was obviously getting the upper hand on Joe, as the older brother, but Joe had no idea why he came after him the way that he did.

At one point they stopped, and Joe yelled at Melvin Jr, "What the #$%^ is wrong with you, man?"

Melvin Jr. responded, "I better not ever see you around him again. He's gonna do something, he's gonna be somebody." He was pointing directly at me. Then he turned and looked at me and his anger became frustration. He said, "You think he's cool, you wanna be like him, he ain't #$%^!! As a matter of fact, get up outta my house and don't come back." I bolted out the door, hopped on my bike, and went home. I never quite understood until later, but I'm sure my cousin Melvin Jr. saw the road my cousin Joe was on and simply wanted to scare me from ever being attracted to that path. Well, it worked.

Today, I would ask myself what kind of relationship my cousin Joe had with his biological father growing up?

Rest in peace, Melvin Jr., Ant, and Joe, you all will be forever missed.

Moments like that define the village, because they are warnings. Those warnings should and would typically come from a father, but when you grow up fatherless, the Heavenly Father will always use somebody to get your attention.

Now, back to my aunts. With these women, the one thing that I can remember about my Aunt Florence Ann is that she was always smiling. My aunt Sharlon, aka "Sugar," had a laugh and a spirit that lit up the whole room. My uncle Nathaniel, who we called,

"Man," wasn't around us very much. He has two sons I don't recall ever meeting, John and Julian.

The last conversation I had with my Uncle "Man," he had watched a highlight video of my son as a kindergartener playing basketball, as he was really good. He called and said, "I just saw this video of your boy, he's something else." I thanked him, and that was the last time we spoke.

Out of this group, within the village, I remain close to my cousin Tasha (daughter of Florence). My Aunt Sugar had her children, too, which also included a Tasha as well as Thomas, Theresa, Tanja, and Terry, and their children and grandchildren remain, so prayers go out to those still with us, and I'll say rest in peace to the others we've lost.

My uncle L.D., the legend, was a great athlete who was well known in my community. One of the best storytellers of all time!! The one thing that I know that I received from my uncle, that I didn't know I needed in my youth, was his constant encouragement. He had a way of making you feel like you were the best in the world, even if the story was embellished a bit. Either way, I loved to hear it. When I look back on it, he was saying things to me that I needed to hear from my own father. Even to this day, when I see him and we spark a conversation, he may say something like, "I remember that time when "Q" was hot, and all I kept hearing the radio station announcer saying was, "Moore hits another one," referencing a basketball game. Maybe the announcer said that, maybe he didn't, but my uncle knew how it impacted me, and that I needed it.

I can remember how thrilled I was when he came to a few of my games over the years. When I was playing little league baseball, he came to a game, and I was playing center field, a ball was smacked to center and I made a jump on it and made a diving, sliding catch, and the small crowd went nuts. When I looked up, all I could see standing there clapping with a smile and a little bit of gold showing in his mouth was my uncle L.D.

He would take us fishing, and Curt, Lil Larry, Rennie, Scott, and myself all piled up in a yellow LTD. To be honest, hunting and fishing weren't my thing, but it's what my uncles loved to do. There was one fishing trip where two things always come to mind. I caught a nine-pound carp and was too weak to bring him in, as I must've been about nine years old. He saw me struggling with it, ran over and said, "Q, you've got a big one!!" I was smiling from ear to ear as he reeled it in and unhooked it. I can remember him holding it up and yelling to someone that he knew, as he knew everybody from everywhere, "Look at what my nephew caught, a nine-pound Carp!" I could care less about the fish; I was just happy that a man who I loved acknowledged me and was both happy and proud of me. I know he never really knew how that made me feel, but it was something that I'll never forget.

The other funny moment from that day that will stick with me forever was when he opened the cooler and asked, "Who drank all of the pop?" For those of you who don't know, where I'm from, soda was called "pop," short for soda-pop. I could hear my cousin, Lil Larry, say, "Rennie drank 'em all," and my uncle looked at my cousin Rennie and said, "Rennie, you've got to enjoy your pop, son." We all laughed, even Rennie, as he always had a huge smile on his face, always. Rest in peace, Ren.

In that moment, I realized that no man had ever called me son before. I'd been called nephew, cuz, and grandson by men, but never a son. It was just another reminder of what I didn't have, but I'm grateful today that I had my uncle L.D. Thanks, Unc.

My cousin, Curt, who was my uncle L.D.'s oldest son, was like an older brother to me. He too had a stint of living with my grandparents at 404 Rocheport St. I looked up to him like most little brothers look up to their older brother. He could've told me that the sky turned red at night, and I would've believed him. He was my example of cool.

One night, he was getting ready to go out on a date. He was telling me about how his date would go and that they were going to the movies. He must've seen in my eyes that I wished I could go with him. As he was about to leave, he said, "Do you wanna go with me?" My big eyes lit up and I said, "YEAH!" I just knew that my grandma would never let me go with him, especially on a date with a girl. Curt was about six years older than me, thus another reason my grandma would probably say no. The time came for Curt to leave, and I had gotten my shoes on and was ready to go, when he walked right out the door and didn't mention anything about me going. I was completely devastated. About thirty seconds later, he came back in the door and said, "Grandma, is it okay if I take Q with me to the show? I'll bring him back after the movie ends."

My Grandma loved her some Curt and replied, "Awww, I don't know."

I looked at her with the big eyes and said, "Please, Grandma..."

Curt jumped in, "He'll be alright Grandma, I won't let nothing happen to him."

She said, "Okay, go get my purse so I can give him some money."

I was so excited, and when we got there, Curt, like any big brother would, said to me, "Now, you go sit near the front where I can keep my eye on you, we'll be sitting in the back." At that time, I had no idea what the back of the theater meant for teenage boys and girls.

Either way, I was happy with my popcorn and candy. To this day, I have no idea what the movie was, as it was simply more important about me tagging along with Curt. Thanks, bruh.

My aunt Kaye is one of the sweetest people on the planet. The story goes that my mother got my name from my aunt Kaye. She had a daughter, my cousin Sheri, who was a couple years older than myself, and she told my mom that if she had a son, she was going to give him my name, so since she had a daughter, my mother took the name. Either way, after I studied the meaning of my name, I knew that my Heavenly Father had selected it all along. Kaye would do anything for anyone. She and my uncle Herman lived in St. Louis, and I would go to visit them, including my cousin Vinnie, in the summers.

Since this ended up being the city that I would end up living in, my relationship with

Kaye would come full circle. As she got older and needed my help for anything, I would hear the voice of my grandmother saying, "Quinny, you do whatever you have to do in order to help Kaye, you hear me?" so I did.

My grandmother told me the story about Kaye and how she was sick at around the age of seven and doctors didn't give her much of a chance to live. My grandma said that she sat in that hospital room the entire time that my aunt Kaye was there, and when the doctors had given up hope, my grandmother did the only thing she could do, she cried out to God. She told me that she made a deal with God and said, "If you save my little girl, I'll never take another drink of alcohol." Kaye is in her seventies today, and my grandmother never took another drink from that moment on. Though we never need to bargain with God because His will is already done, my grandmother's heart was for her child, as all mothers usually are, and obviously the Lord had been dealing with her about her drinking long before that. But He honored her request, as He saw the sincerity and love in her heart. This isn't always the case, as for many it's just their time, whether young or old; however, he spared Kaye's life, and for that, I'm forever grateful.

I truly believe that both my aunt Billie and my aunt Kaye saw me more like a son than a nephew; that was their role within the village. That's just how a village operates, you step into the role that you are needed for at any particular time.

My aunt Kaye's husband, my uncle Herman, was always cool with me, we'd talk sports from time to time, but he had a major impact on my life that needs to be noted in this book.

In the spring of 1993, I made a call to my aunt Kaye, as I knew I wasn't returning for my sophomore year of college, and asked if I could stay with them in St. Louis. I felt like a failure due to how my first year of college turned out and knew that I couldn't go back home.

As I said before, Kaye was one of the sweetest people on earth to me, and she told me that I could stay with them. I was only nineteen years old and had just finished my freshman year in college, packed up the car, and drove to St. Louis. I pulled up into her driveway, excited about this new chapter of my life, got out of the car, saw my aunt in the window.

My uncle Herman came to the door and said, "Now, Quincy, you can't stay here. I have two kids and not enough room in my house as it is." I can remember being floored and angry at the same time. I looked at my aunt in the window as she looked at me, her eyes saying, "I'm so sorry." To this day, I thank

Uncle Herman, because that moment forced me to become a man and learn how to survive on my own.

Another father-to-son moment that I needed came from someone within the village. Rest in peace, Unc.

My aunt Katherine, also known as "Pumpkin," was the strict disciplinarian of the village, but she loved hard and was always loyal to her family, along with her husband, my uncle Bobby, also known as "Fall Guy." I would often hang out at her house because her house was full of kids, LaMonica, Anne, Melvin (Tut), Timmie (T-Bob), Michael (Lukey), Kim, and Cortez. However, I always knew when it was time to go home, as again, they were under very strict regiments that I wanted no part of, so if she ever came to the door looking for one of the kids, that was my signal that it was time for me to go.

I always knew how much she loved me, though. She never had to really say it growing up; I just always knew. We talk more now, as she, too, is in her seventies, and she makes sure that I get the word out for anybody's birthday in the family and asks us to send cards. For me, that's the least we can do.

As I mentioned, she had kids and a few were right around my age, but her son Timmie and I were in the same grade, and when we were in high school, he was my ace, my ride or die; he always had my back no matter what, and because of that loyalty, I always had his, to this day.

One night, I chose to sleep over at their house. There were four boys that slept in one bedroom, with two sets of bunk beds. I slept on one of the top bunks, and at about two in the morning, it had to be 110 degrees in that house. It was miserable, but everybody else was knocked out. I couldn't take it, so I got up and exited the front door and walked home. I lived about three blocks away. Now, it's important to know that I was around twelve years old at the time.

The next morning, I could hear my aunt talking to my mother and I knew that I was in trouble. When I walked into the living room, my aunt let me have it. "Boy, don't you ever do something like that again. Anything could've happened to you, and nobody would've known."

She was right, and I apologized, but what I really wanted to ask was, "Why is your house so hot?" But out of respect, I kept my mouth shut and took it. My mother laughed when I told her why I left. Aunt Katherine was a true pillar in the village.

Then there's my uncle Sam and my aunt Catherine, they were that part of the village that seemed to just always be there.

They had two daughters, my cousins Shonte and Jasmine.

My uncle Sam didn't say a whole lot, but he didn't have to, because I always knew he would protect the family at any cost. You know the old saying, "Watch out for the quiet ones"? Well, that was my uncle Sam. When there were family gatherings at 404 Rocheport Street, the kids were told to play outside, even if the temperature outside didn't have a number, it was just scorching. My grandparents had a screened-in porch that probably sat a good fifteen to twenty feet off the ground, if not more. This particular time, they were having the screen replaced and the old screen had been removed so that space was wide open. All the kids were playing outside, and somebody screamed. I don't believe they were hurt or anything, but just playing as kids, all I can remember is my uncle Sam running out the door and flying through that space on the porch where the screen had been removed, landing twenty feet down on the ground in his cowboy boots, saying, "What's going on out here, who's hurt?"

We all stood frozen, and Shonte assured him, "Everything is fine, Daddy, nobody is hurt."

He replied, "Y'all stop screaming out here."

At that moment, I knew that my uncle Sam would fight or even die for his family, but I also thought to myself how I had never used the word daddy toward anyone. I thought he was like a superhero when I saw him come flying through the air, it seemed like slow motion when I look back on it.

His wife Catherine was a sweet lady who loved sports. We would talk basketball, especially Michael Jordan and the Chicago Bulls. I believe because of my aunt Catherine, the Lord blessed me with a wife who loved sports too, especially basketball. Rest in peace, Auntie.

Aunt Donna, the one and only!!! The best way that I can describe my aunt Donna is that she has the heart of an evangelist. She will tell the world about Jesus the way that Christ commanded us to do with the Great Commission. God has no doubt about who her heart belongs to, as it truly belongs to Him, her daughter Kizzy, and her grandchildren.

Donna always showed me love for as long as I can remember. Her and her daughter Kizzy may be the tightest knitted mother and daughter duo that I know. I'd like to acknowledge Kizzy for always standing up for and taking care of her mother, it may not have been said enough, but it needs to be recognized. Trust me when I tell you, none of our family events truly began until Aunt Donna arrived.

Goldie and Bobbie, my aunt and uncle, were kind of like "Bonnie and Clyde." My aunt Gloria, who everybody calls "Goldie," was more like my older sister, as we are only fourteen years apart. I was always at their house with their children, Sonya, Leon, and Kelly. Ellie came along much later, after I had moved away. I was like a big brother to them, especially Sonya and Leon. Kelly was a bit younger, so she and my brother Derrick were super tight.

Growing up, I was supposed to protect Sonya, and Leon looked up to me like most little brothers do to their big brother, kind of like I looked up to my cousin Curt.

My uncle Bobbie was a giant, bigger than life. "BJ" was an O.G., and I always knew how much he loved me. He was one of the boldest men that I knew and he didn't care what you thought about him, but if you were family, he had your back no matter what. I can recall an episode that involved my uncle BJ that would have a profound impact on me for the rest of my life.

It was summertime, and I was about to enter my sophomore year of high school. I was just walking toward the projects just to see if any of my boys were out and about. Before I made it there, my uncle BJ drove past me, and once he noticed it was me, he stopped the truck and threw it in reverse. "What's going on, Q, where you going, boy?" Before I could respond, he told me to hop in and take a ride with him. My uncle wasn't one you would say no to, so I hopped into his truck.

He seemed bothered, frustrated, maybe even mad. I knew he couldn't be mad at me because I hadn't done anything, but by his demeanor, I wasn't so sure. He didn't say a word, and my uncle was typically very upbeat and tried to make everybody feel good whenever they were in his presence, so this mood was a bit foreign to me.

We pulled into his driveway, got out of the truck, and walked toward his backyard. He goes on to give me a shove to the back, and as I turn around, he's removing his shirt. Now, where I'm from, if it's one on one, mono y mono, and a man removes his shirt, you know what time it is, it's time to put up or shut up. But this was my uncle, he was shredded up with muscles everywhere. I was afraid from the time I shut the door to his truck. He didn't say anything, but after he took off his shirt, I was terrified.

He went on to say, "I need to know if you can handle yourself. See, I know what all of you youngins are into, and y'all will end up either dead or in jail. So, if you end up going to jail, I need to know that you can handle yourself, now put your hands up."

I looked at him as I could feel the tears welling up in my eyes and said, "I ain't trying to fight you, Unc."

He responded, "Naw, naw, those are the people you're running with, right, you look up to them, right, RIGHT?" I really didn't know where all of this was coming from, and before a tear could fall from my eyes, my uncle dropped his fists, grabbed the back of my head and pulled me into his chest and hugged me.

He said, "You ain't cut out for this, Q. I've been to jail and done a lot worse, but that ain't you. You have a lot going for you, but trouble will find you. It takes seconds for you to get into something that may take a lifetime to get out of."

I was what you would call scared straight. After the encounter with my uncle, I knew that for the first time, I could be somebody, even if my father wasn't in the picture.

The final piece of the village were the people who had an impact on my life as an adult, which for me was nineteen and older.

I have to acknowledge my brothers. These are the individuals who are in my circle. I don't need to name them because as they read this, they know whether they are in that circle or not. Brothers are there through the thick and the thin; no matter the cause, they'll be there with you.

I need to acknowledge the following families, the Enyards, Greens, Bennetts, Yandells, Stemmons', Mastins, Davis', Ross, Scales', and Buresch families. Each one of these families have watched me grow from youth to middle-age and have had a major impact on the man that I've become.

Each one of us has a village, some small and some large, like my own. Either way, there were multiple people, outside of your parents, who played a part in who you are, whether their contribution was large or small, they imparted something to you.

It's important when a piece of your hierarchy is missing, especially when it's your father, that you recognize the impact and value of the village, as many of them saw something in you that maybe you didn't see in yourself. But more than that, they loved you. Nothing can ever take the place of an absent father, but the Heavenly Father is always there and will always send the right people at the right time into your life, with the hope of leading you closer to Him.

Thank you, family.

Chapter Three

Do You Know Who I Am?

Around the age of five, I finally gathered up the nerve to ask my mother where was my father. She happily pulled out her high school yearbook from her senior year and showed me a picture of my father. I pulled out that yearbook all the time, just to get a glimpse of the basketball star. I would also look for pictures of my mother, and none of the pictures that I can remember ever showed her really smiling while she was carrying me. My dad smiled with a smirk, the same way that I do.

Though she never really knew it, I would pull that yearbook out quite often and just look at my parents. They looked like polar opposites of each other.

During the years that I would sneak a peek at her yearbook, we lived in a trailer park. I spent many days wandering around that trailer park, which was full of interesting characters. It's weird how many people I can remember, some I still recall their names and others I can only remember their faces.

Billie and Bobbie were two girls I spent a lot of time with, I believe their mother's name was Alice. There was a guy named Ken and I remember an older couple where the husband could touch his chin to his nose. It always made me laugh. I often hung out at a little general store that was at the entrance of the trailer park. They were really nice to me, and each day I'd come in, they would give me a Hostess fruit pie. When you're that young, you don't know that you're poor or a minority, and innocence is bliss.

When I think back on that time, wandering around that trailer park, I know that my Heavenly Father was with me. He looked out for me, protected me, guided me, talked to me, as my biological father was supposed to do. I could've been abducted, abused, even killed, yet here I am, writing.

When I wasn't wandering around the trailer park, I was looking at that yearbook. My father was a basketball star, and my mother was carrying her first child as a teenager. Your senior year is supposed to be the best year ever, yet my mother looked anything but happy in all the pages that carried pictures of her. In almost every image, she had on a trench coat, surely to hide the fact that she was pregnant. We must remember that this was long before being a teen mom would land you on VH1 or MTV in a reality TV show. My mother looked extremely lonely, I can only imagine the amount of guilt, shame, and condemnation that she felt, not to mention the amount of confusion a seventeen-year-old mind had to be going through during that time. A big part of that confusion was directly connected to my father never taking responsibility for his part in the conception.

My father looked like he didn't really have a care in the world, as I'm sure it was on to the next female. I'm not saying that in an angry way, I'm just being realistic. Teenage males typically don't have the responsibility of caring for a child, thus the boys seem to get the opportunity to simply be "Young and dumb" and basically hear from adults around them, "Don't make the same mistake twice," especially if they're a star athlete.

And then there's that word, "mistake." Though it's mentioned nonchalantly, that term somehow becomes connected to the relationship, the act of sex itself, and ultimately the child. It may never be uttered to the child directly, but trust and believe that at some point in their lives, children who are fatherless will question whether they were a mistake. The answer to that question is always NO! A mistake is buying a low-fat item instead of the normal one, that's a mistake. Having unprotected sex and knowing the possible consequences is a choice, and if you aren't ready to handle those consequences, it usually turns into a bad choice.

If you grew up fatherless, maybe it wasn't a yearbook, maybe it was an old photo that your mother had or some other family member. Maybe it was an old video, and for many, there's nothing, nothing at all. They've never seen a picture and the stories were all negative. When your identity is based upon a yearbook, a photo, a verbal description, or some old video footage, it can be extremely difficult.

There are those whose fathers died unexpectedly, while in their mother's womb or shortly thereafter. Some fathers were sentenced to life in prison while their child was in the womb, a newborn, infant or toddler. These are situations where those previously mentioned items will be helpful, as it may be the only connection they'll ever have to their father. However, if your father is still alive but has refused to be a part of your life, then those items will never truly be enough to suffice the longing for answers and a unique desire for some sort of connection.

When I look back on it now, it was a valuable piece of my history. Having the ability to see him with my own eyes allowed me to piece together my own version of my parents' relationship. I would daydream about what it would be like as a family, the three of us. I thought about playing with him, hugging him, watching TV while in his lap, but those were only dreams, and in the end, that's all I had. There was something about seeing their photos, seeing their eyes, their demeanor, and how it all connected to me. Pictures tend to always give you at least a small piece of the truth, and though I haven't seen those pictures or that yearbook in decades, those photos are forever engrained in my memory, as I'm sure that was always God's intention from the moment He allowed me to see it.

If you have old pictures of your parents, try taking a deep, long look at who they seem to be within those pictures. You may never know the real answer, but I believe that God will give you exactly what you need from them. If you don't have any pictures, I suggest trying to do some digging, as someone has photos of both your mother and your father. I pray that if you've never seen them, you get that opportunity, as there is truly some sort of peace there.

I guess it was around fifth grade when I began to take an interest in basketball. I remembered from Mama's yearbook that my dad was a basketball star, and I'd be lying if that didn't motivate me to play the same sport that he did, but with a deeper desire to be better than him.

That was about the time I was introduced to playing a game of "Bucket," also known as twenty-one or thirty-two. If you've ever played "Bucket," then you know exactly what I'm talking about. From the time that I was able to put that ball through the rim, whether it had a net or not, I wanted to do it as often as I possibly could, and so did everyone around me.

In my neighborhood, everybody pretty much knew everybody. You knew their families, and for many, you even knew some of their family history, at least bits and pieces of it. It was no surprise that everybody typically knew who the fathers were of the kids growing up without them in the home. Sometimes the father may reside right down the street and never have a relationship with their child. There were also situations where people were siblings with the same mother but different fathers in the same neighborhood. Imagine how confusing it must be for a kid to know who his father is but he is married to another woman and lives with her and their kids, while living in angst as to if he even cares that you exist. This was true for a few of us, though it wasn't really until high school when those things were discovered, and like I said, everybody knew everybody, so those family secrets would often become public news.

Around junior high, a group of us got summer jobs working at the local college under the supervision of my cousin Mike, a.k.a. "Easy Money," and Carl, a.k.a. "Lil Joe." That group of us included, by nicknames, Roni, Lõg (long

O sound), Trump (No affiliation with America's 25th President), and T-Bone. We were to assist with any housekeeping chores all over the campus. We would ride around in the back of a pickup truck and thought it was cool, as others had done before us. There was a sense of pride just to be working. Though we clowned around a lot, like kids do. My uncle BJ also worked there, so I knew I had to keep my head on a swivel because if I ever got into any trouble and he got wind of it, that was my behind.

There were so many conversations that were had between us, Easy and Lil Joe. Easy was a gentle-hearted person and real nice guy. He had been a basketball star as well, a year younger than my dad, so he knew him well. One day we got on the topic of basketball, which we would do quite often, and Easy said, "Q, you kind of play like your Pop's. I mean, you remind of him when you're out there playing. You're built like him." I remember my heart skipping a beat because that was the first time I had ever heard anything like that as it related to my father. It caught me off guard, and because I was surrounded by my boys I had to respond as tough as I possibly could in that moment. I said, "Please, that dude didn't show me nothing, this is all me." Looking back on it now, that response didn't really get a response out of anyone else, it was just something that I felt I had to say to keep from letting my true feelings out regarding how I had longed to hear something like that from anybody, and wanted to shout, "Tell me more!"

As I got older, I would hear that quite often from people who knew my father and his game and how similar mine looked to his, though I had never seen him play. Shoot, up until that point, I had never seen him in person or at all. I guess you could add Easy and Lil Joe to the village of people that I mentioned previously, because in those short summer months, they always shed some fatherly advice.

Like I said, Easy was a gentle, kindhearted dude who went on to become a Pastor, which is not surprising. He truly has the heart of Christ. As for Lil Joe, he was kind of quiet, but we all knew not to mess with Joe. He was that disciplinarian that kept all of us knuckleheads in line; well, as much as he could, as I can remember him telling Mike, "Easy, you can't let them do that kind of stuff." When Easy wasn't around, he would correct us the way a father would instruct his own kids, and none of us ever bucked up against it.

Every child who grows up without a father is looking for both guidance and discipline, because those two things for a fatherless child equals out to feel and look like love from a man.

Every now and then, I'll run into Easy, but I haven't seen or talked to Lil Joe in years. If they ever get a glimpse of this book, I want to thank them for loving, guiding, and disciplining us when we needed it.

A few years later, I was talking to Easy, and he told me that one day he was with one of my dad's cousins they called, "Snake," and Snake saw me walking in the distance, my back facing him, and he yelled out my father's name but I didn't respond. He said that Snake yelled it a couple of times until Easy said, "That's Q." When you grow up in the land of the fatherless and people know who your father is, they will typically see the resemblance, and when they feel you're old enough to handle or receive it, I promise that one day you'll hear the words, "Man, you look like your dad." I'm not really in the position to hear that very often since I live in a different city, but I've gone home on several occasions over the years and have heard those exact words. I can remember a few years ago a friend of mine, "Lõg," which is short for Logan, had a wedding reception. I ran into his uncle, who I had known growing up. He looked at me and said my father's first and last name. That was the first time I had ever experienced that.

He asked, "Do you talk to your dad much?"

I responded that we didn't really have a relationship.

People often think that surely you've mended the fences and may even ask how your dad is doing and you have to either respond with a lie or reveal the truth that you don't talk to or have a relationship with him and deal with the look of sadness or that they were sorry that they even brought it up, then reassure them that it's all good, but deep down it's not. It's a wound that still hasn't healed, and when touched, it hurts deeply. The instinct of not letting anyone know how painful it really is becomes automatic, and the cycle of suppression continues. But there is freedom from the cycle, believe me, I know.

It was the winter of my junior year of high school, and our basketball team was ranked seventh in the state. We were in the papers and on the local news, we felt like stars. One night, we played a rival school from our conference at their place. It was nothing out of the ordinary as we had played there a bunch of times, but on this particular night during warm-ups, "Log" came up to me and said, "Hey, I just found out that your Pops is here."

Now, you have to understand what rushed through me in that moment. I couldn't just stop and look around the gym to find him, as I had to stay focused on the game. However, after every layup and rebound, in the layup line, I tried to glance across the gym, but I didn't see him. My heart was pounding so hard that I thought it was going to come out of my chest. That feeling turned into so many different emotions; fear, happiness, anger, but more than any of them, competitiveness. I not only wanted to beat our opponent, I wanted to beat my father, as if he was out there on the court. I wanted him to see and know how good I was and that he had nothing to do with it. I wanted him to see what he missed out on. I wanted him to have a desire for me, but more than that, I wanted him to acknowledge me and to say who I was to him.

As the game went on, I was out of my mind. I was playing so hard, and not in a good way. I was forcing up shots, making terrible, hard fouls, turning the ball over, and trying shots that I wouldn't normally take. I can remember my coach subbing me out, and I knew I was messing up, but I so wanted to tell him not to take me out because my dad was there and that it was the first encounter I had ever had with him, but of course I couldn't tell him that, as he had no clue and was focusing on the game at hand. As I heard the buzzer, I knew the sub was for me.

I walked toward the bench and sat down, and my coach grabbed my arm and said, "What the hell are you doing out there? Get your head in the game!" In all honesty, I wanted to burst into tears because I had no way of expressing what I was feeling. It was so overwhelming that all I could do was try to calm myself down and realize how I was letting my team down by being so selfish. I'm not sure how long I was on the bench, but when I got back in, I just wanted to make plays to help the team come out with a road win, and that's exactly what I did.

When the horn sounded and the game ended, I was walking off the floor, and I felt someone tap me on the shoulder. This was it;

this was the moment I had been waiting my whole life for, and I had no idea how I was about to blow it.

I turned around and there he was, maybe an inch taller than me at that time, but it was him. It was the picture from Mama's yearbook, and he uttered the following words, "Do you know who I am?"

Everything that was cold and hard in my heart came out in my response, "Am I supposed to know who you are?" I thought that made me sound big and bad, though my true feelings were to fall into his arms and cry like a baby, but there was no way that I could ever let that happen. I can remember his eyebrows raising up, as I could tell he was taken aback by my response and the attitude behind it.

As soon as I said that, my cousin Timmie, a.k.a. "T-Bob," who was my ace, my ride or die at that time, the one who always had my back and was always down for whatever, said, "You good, Cuz?" He walked up right beside me, looking at my dad as if to say, "You don't want no problems, man." I smile about that now, because that's just the way it was, as he too grew up fatherless. There was something in that moment that makes me wonder if he sensed what I might've been feeling.

I looked at T-Bob and said, "Naw, I'm good, Cuz."

He went on to the locker room and my dad went on to say, "I'm your father."

I was like, "Aw yeah?" In my mind, I was saying to myself, "Stop trying to act so hard, dummy."

He responded with "I was wondering if maybe we can talk sometime this weekend? Maybe I could swoop you up and we could go to the park or something and just talk?"

I said, "That's cool, I'll meet you at the park on Saturday."

He gave me the time to meet him there, and I walked away with so much joy in my heart. It finally happened, I met my father, and he wanted to hang out with me. I didn't know my stat line or anything, all I knew was that I was going to meet up with my dad in only a few days. I got on the bus, as the ride was forty-five minutes back to the high school, put my headphones on, and my heart was feeling something that it had never felt before.

When I got home, I didn't tell my grandma what happened, and the next time I saw my mom, I didn't tell her either, because I wasn't sure how they might react.

We had agreed to meet that following Saturday around three in the park. As I headed out, walking toward the park, a black Saab pulled up next to me. The passenger side window rolled down and the passenger said,

"Get in, man, we'll give you a ride." As I bent down to see it was my father who was driving. Now, a two door Saab coupe doesn't really have a back seat, but I was able to squeeze in, as for me and my boys, traveling seven or eight deep in a car was normal for us.

The passenger's name was Bernard, who was a friend of my father's and seemed to be more excited than my father about us getting an opportunity to meet. He turned around and said, "So, how does it to feel to finally meet your Pops?"

I didn't really know how to respond, so I just smiled, nodded, and said, "Cool."

He then went on to say, "He's got a surprise for you when we get to the park." My father glanced up into the rearview mirror as he drove.

What I was really thinking was, *How does it feel for him to finally be meeting his son?*

Once we got there, he pulled out a new ball and tossed it to me, saying, "This is for you."

I was like, "Aw, thanks!" I was thinking to myself that this was the first gift that I'd ever received from my dad, and it was a brand-new basketball. I had never had a new basketball before. I'd had a few that were handed down to me, and if I'm being honest, I had snatched a few that may have been laying around in different gyms.

As we got to the court, his friend stood down by the car, and my father began to talk. He said, "You played a good game the other night, you're pretty good. You know, I was a pretty good ball player at that school, too."

I was battling a bunch of emotions, I didn't want to act like some needy kid, but I also wanted him to know that I was truly happy that he came for me. I responded, "Yeah, I sort of heard that."

My dad went on to say, "So, the truth is, your family wouldn't let me see you." Right then and right there, everything changed, because I knew that was a lie. My mother would've never kept him from me, and neither would any of my other family members. They may have tried to protect me, but no one would ever prevent him from seeing me or having a relationship with me. He went on to tell me how I had a whole other family that he wanted to introduce me to in due time. He gave me his address and his phone number. He asked if I'd be able to take a trip with him. It was really happening, and it was happening fast, too. We shot around for a little bit, and after about thirty or forty-five minutes, I told him that I needed to get going. I really didn't, but things were starting to get a bit awkward for me. I couldn't really get past him saying that my family wouldn't let him see me. Throughout the entire time, I never heard him say my name.

He would always refer to me as, "Young Man." "You played well last night, young man. You're almost as tall as me, young man." That kind of thing.

When I got home, I told my grandmother where I had been and who I was with and she sort of looked down, nodded, and said, "You need to tell your mama." That was pretty much it, there was no excitement or anything, and then I began to wonder if they had forbid him to see me.

The next time I was at my mom's house, I told her where I had gone and who I was with, and she kind of freaked out. I couldn't understand why she was so upset, saying, "So, you go hang out with him after he's never wanted anything to do with you?" I was so confused, I thought she would be happy for me. I couldn't understand why neither my mom nor my grandmother showed any happiness for me, and then it hit me; they were scared, and they didn't want to see me get hurt.

I took my mom's outrage about it all and let it be. Nothing was going to deter me from seeing him, as I had been waiting for this my whole life.

Over the next few weeks, my dad and I were hanging kind of tough. He came and picked me up to have dinner with him and his girlfriend at the time. It was a nice apartment, and she was super nice to me. We talked about a lot of things that night, and I could feel myself getting comfortable. As we sat there, I started thinking about my dad's car, his apartment, and thought how he must have money. About a week after that, he drove me to the city where his father lived and took me to see him. He introduced me as his son, but not by my name.

His father was older, and he didn't have a big response to it, but he asked me some questions about my family and then he and my father held a longer conversation. After they talked, we left and headed back home. I thought it was cool, but I have to be honest and say that it wasn't the reception that I thought I would've received when I met my grandfather for the first time. No fault to him, as he acted like he had no clue that we were going to be there anyway and he didn't know anything about me. I didn't read much into it, as I was happy just being in the presence of my dad.

About a week later, he wanted to take me shopping for some shoes. Now, we didn't have much, but by this time, I was getting every pair of Air Jordans, as my mother and grandmother would spoil me. I wasn't going to ask him for some Jordans, but I knew of a pair of shoes that I wanted, and if they were still in the Foot Locker, I was going to ask for those. Once we got to Foot Locker, they were still there, some bright blue Nike Forces.

He picked them up, and I will never forget his response, "NINETY DOLLARS! I'M NOT PAYING NINETY DOLLARS FOR SOME SNEAKERS!" And there it was, a part of being a parent that he wasn't prepared for; financial support.

My mood changed immediately after that, and I said, "You don't have to buy me any shoes, man. I usually where Jordan's, like the ones on my feet, and they cost more than those. You offered to buy me shoes and asked which ones I wanted, so I told you."

He replied, "I had no idea sneakers cost this much money, and I just can't do it. I'll find you some other ones and send them to you."

I told him, "It's cool, I don't need any, it's fine."

He went on to say, "No, no, I wanted to get you some shoes and I'm gonna get you some shoes."

Talk about awkward. After that interaction, I didn't say much and was ready to go. I knew we had planned to go back to his girlfriend's apartment again, but by this time, I started to get bad thoughts and was like, *I'm going to stir up this situation.*

We got back to his girlfriend's apartment, and I told her what happened. He went on about how he just couldn't see paying that much for shoes for a sixteen-year-old.

I then blurted out to his girlfriend, "Hey, do you think I could use your car?" The shock on their faces were priceless, and she didn't really know how to respond. I didn't expect for them to say yes, but I wanted them, more so my dad, to understand that this was a part of having a teenage son. He had missed the newborn, toddler, child, and adolescent years. I wanted him to know what kind of things I had already experienced in life without him, both good and bad. However, I didn't go into anything else and just sat back for their response about using the car with a smirk on my face.

My father said, "She doesn't feel comfortable letting you use her car, as you're only sixteen and she barely knows you."

I responded with, "It's cool, I was always told that you never know until you ask."

I was trying to understand what my father was trying to do; did he really think he could just walk into my life and be a dear old dad? Surely, he didn't think that, but the reality was, he didn't think of what it took to really be a father. There's so much more to the role than simply showing up and trying to be there or bringing gifts.

That night ended rather quietly, and I was dropped off at my grandma's house. The previous times he had dropped me off, he said something like, "I'll try to see when the next time we can hook back up." However, this time, he simply said, "I'll be in touch." It felt different and colder, and I thought that I must've offended him.

After not hearing from him for a few days, he called to let me know that he was stopping by to drop off some shoes. He dropped off a pair of black Nike sneakers that looked like shoes a referee would wear, something that I would never wear. Call me ungrateful, and maybe I was, but it felt like a cheap gesture. They probably cost no more than forty bucks.

I said, "Ah, thanks."

He asked, "You like 'em? I got black because you can wear those with anything."

I responded, "Yeah, they're cool." I was grateful for the gift but was disappointed in what he bought. But again, I had been spoiled. He didn't stay around long and drove off, and that was that, or so I thought.

After he left, I got the sense that things were changing from the time we spoke at the park. I felt as if he wasn't really prepared to be a father, even though his first-born son came onto the earth close to seventeen years prior to the day he met him. It seemed that the responsibility of being a father was a bit overwhelming. Imagine that. There was still hope in my heart that a relationship would develop between the two of us though. After all, it had only been a little over a month since we'd met.

About a week or so after my father dropped off the shoes that he had bought for me, I hadn't heard from him. I had his number, but this was a time when there were no cell phones and you had to call from a landline, and where he lived it would be a long-distance phone call. I didn't want to hear anything about who I was calling if I asked to make a long-distance phone call, yes, you had to ask to call long distance, so, I decided to wait.

A few days went by, and a Fed-Ex truck pulled up in front of my grandma's house. Now, you must understand that a Fed-Ex truck pulling up where we lived did not happen very often, if ever. Every blue moon, a UPS truck may appear, but never a Fed-Ex truck. It was nothing like it is today, as you may see a Fed-Ex, UPS, or Amazon truck every other day in your neighborhood.

I met the driver at the door, and he handed me a Fed-Ex envelope addressed to me. In my mind, this had to be my first recruit letter for basketball. I mean, who else would send me something by way of Fed-Ex?

I sat down and ripped it open. It was a handwritten letter from my father. In a nutshell, the letter claimed that he never really had a relationship with my mother, and he never got a paternity test. He went on to apologize for the confusion but ended the letter by saying there's no way I could be your father. I was numb, so I put the letter back into the envelope, balled it up, and stuffed it at the bottom of the trash so that no one would find it.

It would be years before I ever told anyone about that letter. I never told my grandmother, and I probably didn't tell my mother until I was in my late twenties or early thirties. I buried it, and I also buried him with it. Well, at least I thought I did.

Something happened in that moment that is difficult to explain. Picture a heart, whether a picture of it or the actual organ, now picture it gradually going coal or onyx black in a matter of seconds. That was what happened to my heart. I was deep into listening to "Gangsta Rap" music, and at that moment, I grabbed my Walkman and tossed in Ice Cube's, "Amerikkka's Most Wanted" cassette tape.

The album came out about a year before that, and I had pretty much memorized the whole thing. I rewound it to the first song on side one, which was titled, "The N!@@# You Love to Hate."

In this book, I vowed to keep it as real as I possibly could to show the impact a father has, whether in or out of the life of his children. In that song, the very first verse says, "I heard payback a m#!@%^&*^%#@! N!@@#, that's why I'm sick of getting treated like a g.d. stepchild, f#!@ a punk cause I ain't him, you gotta deal with the nine-double-m."[8] These lyrics were tattooed on my heart, right before it turned black, and from that moment on, everything changed, and I would be heading on a downward spiral to destruction.

---

8 Ice Cube, "Amerikkka's Most Wanted." 1990.

Chapter Four

The Birth of Bitterness, Anger, and the Darkness of Destruction

---

Biblical studies often explain how Lucifer (Satan) was the angel over worship or music. In my mind, he was the ultimate worship leader. Though he was cast out of heaven, he didn't lose his ability to influence within his God-given gift of music. This is my belief.

Think about it, how awesome and powerful is music? It can make you feel happy, sad, even mad, now that is some real powerful stuff. I consider myself to be a music head and love all kinds of music, but during this time in my life, the influence of music was constantly flowing through my ears, straight to my now blackened heart, and from there bitterness was born.

Bitterness is defined as "Anger and disappointment at being treated unfairly; resentment."[9] All of us have experienced being bitter at one time or another. The problem with bitterness is that it can linger on and on, sometimes for a lifetime. This is where problems will arise, and it's not a matter of if, it's a matter of when and to whom you'll take it out on, usually it's the ones closest to you that you will hurt the most.

I wasn't aware that bitterness had crept into my heart after my heart had gone completely dark. But I began to change. I developed an ability to cut people off if you ever crossed me, just like I did with my own father. What little relationship that had begun with my him was now done, in my mind and in

---

9 merriam-webster.com

my heart. He couldn't say anything to me at that moment. I felt this anxiousness not to let people get too close, and if I'm being totally honest, a little bit of that still resides in me today. I understand now that it was a protection mechanism, as there was a fear of letting someone in and them leaving me, so I either kept them at bay or waited for them to cross me, and if they did, that was it. Bitterness has had an impact on nearly every relationship that I've ever had, and when I take a deeper look at it, that's a sad and sorry way to live.

Out of bitterness will typically come anger. I have battled anger for as long as I can remember. However, after the letter that I received from my father, the anger became something like never before. This time, it was dark and destructive. I often felt like a ticking time bomb. To be honest, it's a scary feeling, because you are so uncertain of what you may be capable of doing. For those who are closest to me, they have witnessed this firsthand, and it's not a pretty sight or something that I'm proud of.

I often say that I have a gamma problem. If you are familiar with The Incredible Hulk, you know that he was a product of a gamma ray experience that went bad and every time he became angry, he turned into the Hulk. This huge, super strong, green colored individual would tear up anything in his path. In the late 70s and early 80s, *The Incredible Hulk* was a TV show. During the opening of the show, David Banner said, "Mr. McGee, don't make me angry, you wouldn't like me when I'm angry."[10] Once the Hulk made an appearance, there was no turning back. He didn't count to ten or take deep breaths. No, the wrath was coming, and that was often how I carried myself. And if I'm being honest, it still rears its ugly head if I'm

---

[10] "The Incredible Hulk." Universal Television. 1977.

not careful or if I'm disconnected from my Heavenly Father.

You have to understand that it would take years before I would truly understand that the root of it all was fatherlessness.

It's true that hurt people hurt people. That doesn't give people an excuse to cause harm, but I can tell you, as it relates to me, from anger came the darkness of destruction. The people who usually were the closest to me would experience some form of it. Whether it was mental, emotional, and in some cases physical, but if my anger was ever at its highest point, destruction was somewhere nearby. Think about how much destruction the Hulk would cause.

This whole thing with my father had become a tornado within my soul, and it was out to destroy any and everything in its path, with the ultimate goal of destroying me. The sad part about all of this is that I was more than willing to let it.

One of my favorite books of the bible is the book of James. There is a well-known passage of scripture that comes from James 5:16 that says *"Therefore, confess your sins to one another and pray for one another, that you may be healed. The prayer of a righteous person has great power of a righteous person has great power as it is working."*[11]

It is definitely the prayers of the righteous, along with God's grace and mercy, that allows me to still be here and write this book.

The fact that I was now broken, bitter, and my heart had grown darker than ever, when you add all those things together, it can only lead to

---

[11] Unless otherwise noted, all biblical passages referenced are in the ESV Student Study Bible, Crossway Books (2011).

destruction, and that's exactly where I was heading.

Nothing really mattered. Yeah, I continued to be a pretty good student, a basketball player, and a decent person, but I just didn't care. I no longer cared about people's feelings.

At that point, my circle became even smaller since my cousin Scott, who was like my big brother growing up, was off to college. He had been watching over me for as long as I could remember, and now he was gone. Looking back on it now, I could be a pretty mean and cruel individual. Making fun of people, causing them pain for my entertainment and those around me. Never really thinking about how they felt or how deep what I was saying about them was hurting them at their core. Nine times out of ten, you would make fun of people to keep others from making fun of you. Like I said before, hurt people hurt people. I was hurting and causing destruction to as anyone who happened to be in my path.

I pray that if anybody that I hurt reads this book, they would please forgive me.

On the inside, fear was growing, and I simply wasn't going to allow anyone to hurt me again. If you weren't loyal or if you ever crossed me, I had a mechanism deep in my soul that could and would cut you off just like that. Even if it was family, as family played a role in putting me in this position; my biological father. Even as I write this, reliving that pain, is still hard to walk through, but I hope it helps someone who may be still there because of how the absence of their father has affected them. Trust me when I tell you, you are not alone, and I feel you, believe me, I feel you. Let me reassure you, there is light at the end of the tunnel for you, too, and I'm going to show you how to obtain it.

Believe it or not, promiscuity ties directly into the life of those who grew up without a real relationship with their biological father. I became sexually active around the age of thirteen, not ready in any way for that step. The desire for sex became stronger and stronger after the first time. I once heard my pastor say that the two strongest desires for mankind are food and sex. The father of the home is supposed to be the example of how a man should treat a woman and the kind of man a young lady could see herself marrying one day. The problem is that without the example of the father in the home, the door is left open to be influenced by anyone and anything. For me, it was cousins, both boys and men in the neighborhood, especially those who seemed to have a lot of women. Sure, I had my grandfather, but he was an older man by the time girls became a real interest. My uncles were married to my aunts, but I wasn't with them on a daily basis. My stepfather was there, but he worked overnight and slept during the day. So, like I said before, there were my cousins and the fellas in the neighborhood.

There was a major element that drove the desire through the roof, and it was my introduction to pornography. Now, I had seen rated R movies that had nude or sex scenes, but nothing close to what porn revealed. My cousin had access to what we called, "The Vault." It was a large collection that was owned by his father, and we were addicted to it. Our eyes were opened to things that we never knew were possible. In the summer when all our parents were working in the day, I would get a phone call from my cousin, simply stating, "The vault is now open." We would spend hours watching, and sometimes we had all dudes from the hood in his house. So, now you have a bunch of teenage boys with their hormones going out of control, and the only thing on their minds was how to do what we just saw those men doing on the TV. There was nothing about love, relationships, or anything else, it was nothing but sex.

At that time, there was nothing in us that thought any of the people could possibly be acting, only having the time of their lives.

The mindset at that time was to seek out any girl that may be willing to experiment with sexual activity. That being said, let's take a look at this from a young teenage girl's perspective.

God created a natural attraction between male and female; however, the enemy took that attraction and perverted it into something that was intended and created for married people but was now just a physical act that was extremely pleasurable and euphoric.

With teenage hormones raging out of control, and never having the sex talk with my father, that only equals troublesome and unexpected situations. Many of those situations lead to the same situation as my own. Young parents, and more times than not, a child without a father. This process will typically begin with promiscuity.

To be honest, I have had sex with many females, and two different females became pregnant and had abortions. Some may wonder why I added that to the book, and the reason is because I know that there is someone who will read this and see themselves in what I am describing, and I want them to know that it has a direct connection to fatherlessness. If so, I just want them to know that they aren't alone, and if you're struggling to forgive yourself, I'm living proof that there's forgiveness at the cross for all of mankind.

Becoming promiscuous during one's adolescent years is as common as facial hair for men and menstrual cycles for women; it's going to happen. When this time occurs for parents, most father's will stand proud for their sons and shaking in their boots as it pertains to their daughters.

Having three daughters and one son, my wife and I tried to split "The Talk." She would talk to the girls, and I would talk to my son. I'm not sure if that really holds weight or not, as I believe the true teacher is allowing them to witness how a man treats a woman from the father's example and how the woman treats a man from the mother's example. Since all parents are human, those two examples can end up being extremely flawed, since parents are far from perfect.

We are all products of our environments, so the more we attempt to be the opposite of our parents, the more we sound just like them. Though some people grow up in environments that seemed like hell, for the most of us, if we think hard enough, the good probably outweighed the bad, and if we look at the environments that our parents come from, it just might make sense why they were the way they were, even if they were absent. That's never an excuse, but believe me, it plays a part. If you had halfway decent parents that weren't perfect but tried to love you the best way they knew how to love, consider yourself blessed.

Previously, I mentioned how I was introduced to pornography and how that jumpstarted the engine of promiscuity. Today, pornography is easier to access than ever before, so that jumpstart is happening at much younger ages, and when you add the impact of social media, you'll find promiscuity at an all-time high.

There are more cases today of rape, incest, and molestation than ever before. There are websites where you can find people that could be living in your neighborhood and are listed as a sex offender. Predators are lurking on the internet seeking out our children.

1st John 2:16 reads, *"For all that is in the world – the desires of the flesh and the desires of the eyes and pride of life – is not from the Father but is from the world."*[12] The Bible is full of many warnings, and many of us live our lives ignoring them.

My teenage years had a major impact on what kind of father I would become.

My wife had two daughters when we got married. I was more than aware of the world in which I lived and never wanted an opportunity for a situation to arise where anyone could ever accuse me of doing something inappropriate with them sexually. So, I didn't hug them a lot and never kissed them on the forehead or the cheek like a father will often do with his children, some directly on the mouth, especially during the infant and toddler years. I simply didn't want anything to be deemed as perverted. Though my caution may have been wise, warranted, and

---

[12] Ibid.

commendable, it's also very sad, because those little girls needed that from their dad and didn't get it. I think it caused issues with how close our relationships would ever become.

The reason for this is because when my biological children were born, I hugged and kissed all over them, they slept on my chest or laid with me on the couch, and during those times, I didn't realize how my older daughters must've felt. It breaks my heart today, and I know it had a major impact on them, as they needed to be hugged, kissed, and coddled by a father. They deserved that, and it wasn't until they were older that I came to the realization as to how much they needed it. If my two older girls ever read this, please accept how sorry I am and how another opportunity to pour into your life was missed. Man, I hate the devil.

After the Fed-Ex truck arrived at my grandmother's house and I received the letter from my father, my heart and soul turned black.

Like most kids, I had a dream of one day becoming a professional athlete, an NBA player, to be exact. I held onto that dream, even though I was nowhere near good enough to become a professional athlete. I've always been and still am a dreamer.

However, after receiving that letter, I was introduced to the realities of life, and one of those realities included no longer holding out for my dream. I had refrained from drinking alcohol and smoking anything up until that point, but it was time to see what the big thing was about drinking. To be honest, I hated the taste of beer. This was pretty much the drink of choice for teenagers, because it was cheap and easy to get someone to purchase it. The year was 1991 and the common drink involved a 40oz, and the cheapest possible brand. I can remember being introduced to malt liquor, "Old-E," and "Big Mouth's" were typically acquired. Malt liquor sent me on a spin quicker than regular beer, and that was the feeling that we all seemed to desire. Under the influence of alcohol, everything seemed funnier, I didn't think about what was constantly dwelling in my mind as it pertained to my father, so I wanted to drink more often. However, alcohol would increase the opportunity to become violent.

Fast-forward to the fall of 1992, and I was a freshman in college. I attended a freshman orientation, and there I would meet a new friend who turned into one of my brothers, D-Lova.

The first thing he asked me when we met was, "Do you drink?" I knew then that college was going to be full of kickin' it.

I lived in Shannon Hall, which we all called "The Ghetto" because it was the worst dorm on campus. My freshman year college clique, a few I'm still in contact with today, included Freddy B, Dre, J-Hard, Big John, Pretty boy Jim, Huls, and Simmons.

One day, I was going downstairs, and I got to the first floor and wandered into the room of an Asian friend of mine named Taka. He had a Super Nintendo and asked if I wanted to play a game. I wasn't really all that interested in video games. I mean, I liked playing them, but I wasn't a gamer.

When I sat down, Taka looked over at me and said, "Q, you wanna smoke?"

In the past, I had always said no to smoking weed, but by this time I had become engulfed by darkness.

I looked over at Taka and said, "Yep."

After the first time I smoked weed, I didn't feel a thing, I can remember thinking how it was all a big hype. A few weeks after that, I was chillin' in my boy's room, "B-Luke." He closed the door and laid a towel at the base of it, and we began to smoke some weed. This time it was different, I felt something.

B-Luke and I enjoyed the same kind of music, and I had never heard the music sound as good as it did after getting high. I can remember becoming extremely charged and angry while listening to the Geto Boys.

All I could think about was how much I hated my father and if he had been in that room, I would've put my hands on him for real. The rage that was inside of me was growing at a rapid pace.

Today, you hear a lot about self-medicating, and beginning in my teens and battling it off and on throughout my adult life, I seemed to always revert to alcohol and weed, and those two combined, where I'm from, was called, "Perved." In my early twenties, I was introduced to the state of mind while being drunk and high. There are so many other names connected with this, but I must say nothing silenced the voices that would become extremely loud in my head. It had the ability of providing me with a false sense of feeling great and special, while in the next moment telling me that I wasn't worth anything and was one of the lowest and saddest cases of human life. The final statement from the voices would always be, "I mean, your own father didn't want you." Let me tell you, it doesn't get any worse than that. When I would enter this abyss of darkness, there was no telling what I was capable of. There were times when I believed I was having running conversations with Satan himself.

So many people were hurt during the moments of self-medicating, including myself. Everybody was fair game to feel the wrath during the time that my heart was overcome with darkness. The people who were hurt the most were the people who were always closest to me or loved me the hardest.

I believed that I must be cursed, and when I was under the influence, the devil had no problem with convincing me that I was right. I was lost.

Picture yourself in a dark, unfamiliar place. It's pitch black and you can't even see your hand in front of your face. Fear is overwhelming, and panic is quick to follow.

Once, during the season of self-medicating, I began to have nightmares that there were black shadows hovering over me and I couldn't move at all as they closed in. There was a struggle and a panic to try to fight and wake up, almost to a point where I couldn't breathe. I would wake up gasping for air. These dreams were happening night after night for about a six week stretch. I didn't want to go to sleep and would have to self-medicate.

I reached out to my mother, and she told me that I needed to schedule a meeting with Bishop Long, who was her pastor at the time. Though I was against it, I was desperate for help, and so I went to see him. Once I was in his office and told him about the nightmare, he looked at me with a grin and said, "Well, that's an easy one, the devil is trying to kill you." It had never felt more real that my life was in real jeopardy. It wasn't but a few hours after meeting with Bishop Long, I went right back to the darkness that I knew and grabbed "The drank and the dank." It was like I wanted to end the suffering, end the turmoil, and the only question that I had was for my father; "Why, Man?"

Even after I accepted Christ and was walking with the Lord, whenever times got really hard, I would always revert back to the way I had always self-medicated. I would talk and listen to God, but when the pain was unbearable, I would always give in to what I knew best. Of course, I would do this in secret so that no one would know what I was doing, but I'm not sure how much of it went unseen. I'm sure my wife knew what was going on, as when I would go into these modes, it always led to a disconnect from God. I felt like I let my Heavenly Father, my family, and myself down, and I would once again hear the voices that would tell me how worthless I was and that I would always be this way and that there was really no hope for me. During these times, the anger would ramp up, and because of how I felt about myself, anyone who came into my path was a target.

Again, hurt people hurt people.

I never wanted anyone to know that I was walking around in pain, as I was prone to never showing any kind of weakness. Whenever I turned to self-medicating, it was always temporary and I needed more to stay in that mode. At one point, it truly began to take a toll on my health. I was a mess.

During this time in my life, I found out that I had two brothers. I went on a search for the older of the two, found him on Facebook, and sent him a friend request. Months went by, and then one day I saw that he had accepted my friend request.

I proceeded to message him directly and asked, "If I were to give you a phone number, would you call it?"

He replied, saying, "Probably not."

I responded by saying, "What if I said that I was your brother?"

He quickly asked, "Number?"

We ended up talking, and I found out that he was around the age of my second daughter. We swapped photos of us when we were younger, and it was scary how much we looked alike. He was super excited, but I knew that this excitement was going to be short lived once my father got involved. He lived with his dad, my father, and saw him to be a real good man, and I didn't want to ruin that for him. He told me that his dad was coming in and he just had to tell him.

We got off the phone, and there was that feeling again, the same feeling that I had when I found out that my father was at my game. A few minutes later, he sent me a message saying, "My dad told me to tell you to never contact him or me again. Get the paternity test."

It felt like receiving the Fed-Ex letter all over again.

As I began to spiral out of control once again, this time the trauma was different. I began to get headaches more and more often. I would have to ask my wife to squeeze my trapezoid muscles as hard as possible and apply pressure to my head in order to relieve the pain. This went on for quite some time, and then I found out that I was battling hypertension. My doctor prescribed me medication for my high blood pressure, yet my self-medicating began to ramp up once more.

One day as I waited for my children to get home from school, I had been self-medicating, and my left arm began to surge and there was tightness in my chest. I became overwhelmed with fear and thought maybe I was having a heart attack. I thought about the possibility of me collapsing and maybe even dying, but worse than that, my children finding me.

During one of the darkest, most disappointing moments in my life., making life-altering decisions, and though I was near the bottom of myself, the Lord allowed me to be blessed with my baby girl.

I always let her know that she was sunshine in my life during an extremely dark time, to nobody's fault other than my own.

I do not blame my father for my choices, but when it came to self-medicating and me feeling like I could stroke out and die, I knew I had to stop. I thought about my wife having to explain how I died and how selfish it was for me to keep putting myself in that situation and the impact it would have on my wife, my children, my mother, my grandmother, and anyone else who loved me.

For once, I decided to think about somebody other than myself.

I've been clean from the "Drank and dank," actions and mentality since that point, but the consequences of my actions still lingered, as the damage had already been done.

Chapter Five

The One

The question is always posed, "How do you know if a person is the one for you?" If you ask me that question, my answer is simple, God will tell you. Now, many people may not truly believe that, but again, that's my answer.

It was 1997 when we met. We worked at the same place, she was a supervisor, and I had just started working there. At the end of the first week, the company would hold sort of a graduation for making it through new employee orientation. The people who were in your class and all the supervisors.

We were introduced, and she said, "Do I know you, you look familiar?"

Though my response was, "No, I don't think so," I heard a voice in my head that sounded like Jack Nicholson as the Joker in the 1989 Batman movie, "Stop the press, who is that?"

She was beautiful and you could just tell it was natural. She didn't need a bunch of makeup or anything, it was God-given. Though she and I were both dating other people at the time, I can't speak for her, but I wanted to know more about her.

To be honest, I sort of stalked her, in a good way. Whenever I would take my break, I would walk toward her desk, just to see if I would run into her. When I did, I'd stop and say hello and try to spark a conversation. I only had fifteen minutes for my break, and when we talked, it seemed like fifteen seconds. I'd be lying if I said that I wasn't attracted to her physically, I already mentioned that, but when we talked, it was like everything she said was tapping into my soul. I had never felt that before with anyone.

Like I said, we were both dating other people, but it was kind of obvious, we were feeling each other.

During that summer, the company that we worked for had an employee day at an amusement park. I was with the girl that I was dating, and of course our paths crossed, and she was with the guy she was dating. There were so many people there, but as our paths crossed, we acted as if we didn't know each other, but when our eyes met, we were locked in with one another for a good five seconds or so. I knew at that moment, somehow, someway, I was going to get to know her better.

Months passed, and by that time the passer-by conversations became less and less due to conflicting schedules. However, when we did come across one another, you could feel the excitement between us. I was so happy to see her but never really had time to talk like we used to. Word had gotten back to me that she was no longer dating her boyfriend. As for me, I had accepted that my current relationship was coming to an end as well.

The company had a Christmas event, and I was going to attend with my girlfriend at the time. Though I knew that relationship was pretty much done, I didn't want to go to the event alone. While sitting with my co-workers at a table, laughing and talking while music was playing in the background, a moment occurred that I will remember forever. As I sat there having a conversation with my co-workers, I felt a tap on my back right shoulder. No one else seemed to notice, and as I turned over my right shoulder, I didn't see anyone, and then I turned over my left shoulder, and walking away, there she was. Our eyes met, and she put up a small wave. She had a smile, but I sensed a sadness in her eyes that really pulled me in even more. It was like she had some sort of spotlight behind her that made her illuminate or something. I guess you could say, it was her aura.

My night would not be the same after that, as I had to end the relationship with the girl I was seeing. Though the break-up was a bit ugly, all I wanted to do was pursue this young lady who was intriguing more than the physical part of me, tapping into something deeper in my soul.

After inquiring about what shift she was working, I thought that the easiest way for me to get closer, to just come back up to the job during whatever hours she was working. The job was literally five minutes away from my apartment. After about my third time popping in and having twenty-minute conversations with her each time, I think she got the picture, so I went ahead and asked for her phone number. The time wasn't like it is now, everybody didn't have a cell phone, so I had to wait to talk to her from our home phones.

The first time we had a conversation, I knew that I was talking to a woman. She was so deep and insightful, and we talked about everything; our upbringings, our families, our hobbies, the job, our futures, her children, and for the first time that I could ever remember, I had a conversation with a young woman about the things of God. She often would counter things that I would say as I would talk about how I liked to go out and kick it with my boys. She wasn't into that, as she had two children, so they were her priority, which meant if I was going to be with her, I was going to have to grow up fast.

Where we worked, they were always having some sort of contest and giving out free items. In one particular contest, I won a dinner for two at a fancy restaurant. I'll put it this way—it was a restaurant that I hadn't been to before and I haven't been to since. However, I thought this was a way that I could impress her, because I was broke, and so I asked if she would have dinner with me. She agreed, and it was our first date. When we got our food at this really nice restaurant, we looked at each other and laughed. It was like three small portions of something we didn't know anything about. Her laugh was contagious, and she was so dang beautiful.

She wanted to know about me, she was interested in me and my story. I was able to make her laugh, and it was refreshing to be able to talk about things that I hadn't really shared with anyone. Something was happening here, and it was only our first date.

Fast forward about a year, and we were a couple. My relationship with her two daughters was, growing and it felt like I had a family.

I went to her apartment one evening in June, and when I walked in, she had the NBA Finals on the TV, and I thought, *She's the one.* A woman after my own heart, as she was a fan of basketball, too.

Everywhere we went, she would run into somebody that she knew. A few of them would tell me, "She was really good at basketball," another vital element added to our connection. As I sat on the couch watching the game, she was cooking dinner and talking on the phone while the girls were playing in their room, and I heard a voice say to me, as clear as if sitting next to me, say, "This is your family."

To be honest, it freaked me out. She looked over as if to say with her eyes, "Are you okay?" I nodded, but I was spooked.

Then the questions began to roll through my mind, *Are you ready for this, a self-made family?*

I went home and called my grandma and told her about this girl that I believed was the one, telling her that she had two children and that I wasn't sure if I was ready for that.

My grandma responded, "Mhm, I know what you mean, it takes a special man to step in and play the father role for children that aren't his, like your grandpa did with me." She always knew how to slip in exactly what I needed to hear. I had completely forgotten that my grandmother had three children when she married my grandfather. She went on to say, "I believe that you could be a special man, too, if she's really the one."

Since it had been over a year and a half, I had a new position where I was making more money than I had ever made, and even though I hated the job, I loved the money. One month,

I had my highest commission check ever, so I decided to go out and buy an engagement ring. It was perfect, and I thought that it shined like her and how she deserved it. I was just hoping that she would say yes.

Though I consider myself to be somewhat creative, I had no clue as to how I was going to propose. So, I decided to transform my small apartment, in the living room area, into what I thought could be heaven on earth. My walls were white, so I hung brand new white sheets along the walls and windows and laid white sheets all along the floor, placing a table for two in the center of the room. Finally, I covered the floor with rose petals.

She walked in and was really surprised, I'm not sure if she knew what was going on or not, but after dinner, I got down on one knee and proposed. She said, "Yes."

I could write a book on our life together, maybe I will one day. We finally got married after a breakup and another proposal. During our wedding, in the front row, her parents sat on the left and my parents on the right. Afterward I told her that I felt like Jesus was sitting in the center of both of them.

The wedding was spirit-filled and overcome with emotion as the anointing flowed like I had never seen before that point. I'm not making that up, you had to be there. You maybe haven't heard the phrase, "People being slain in the Spirit." Directly after our wedding, as the wedding party exited the sanctuary, the entire wedding party began to weep, I mean sobbing, it was uncontrollable. It wasn't sadness but overwhelming joy. I had never experienced anything like that before that time, and I can't say that I've ever experienced it again. We had people who gave their lives to Christ at the end of our wedding.

A couple years later, we welcomed our son, and three years following that, we welcomed our youngest daughter. There were so many trials and tribulations, fun times and heartache, yet she remains, and the only thing that I can say to that is, "Thank you for staying with me."

We have now been married for over twenty-two years. There wasn't then, and there isn't now, any doubt as to who she was and is in my life. She's "The One."

Once I had found "The One," I followed her to the church that she was attending, Metro Christian Worship Center, also known as MCWC. This became our spiritual home and our spiritual family. The first time I attended a service, I heard the Pastor speak, and it felt like he was talking specifically to me. There was an immediate connection to this man, though at that time, we had never met or been introduced, it was just something that I felt on the inside of me.

After we became members of the church, I wrote a letter to Pastor Ray. I expressed how I felt a deep connection to him and that it was far deeper than anything I had ever felt with any other man. It was hard for me to really say what I wanted to say, but I did, I asked if he could be my spiritual father. I understood that he had children of his own, and I respected that he was the leader of a large flock, but I was hoping that the connection was mutual, and once that was confirmed, a real father-son relationship would occur. It was more like the relationship of a father and his adult son. I always respected his family and the role that he served, so I tried not to overstep my bounds, though there would be so many times that I desperately needed to reach out but didn't. In those moments, I had to learn how to talk with my Heavenly Father instead, as no one could ever know me or know what's best for me better than Him.

As a member of MCWC, my children would grow up there, we would serve there in so many different capacities. We would see so many lives changed, so many lives lost, so many souls won, and so many hearts broken, including our own. When you think about it, that's life. The only difference is that all our spiritual family members believed that Jesus Christ was our Lord and Savior. The harsh reality is that, though that may be true, we are still human, and all of us would fall short of the glory of God, which again comes straight from Romans 3:23.

When the human side of people is revealed, their flaws will also appear, and this is when people will usually get hurt. There are expectations for those who claim to be followers of Jesus Christ, and there should be, but many times, those expectations are unrealistic, and finding out someone isn't perfect can be devastating. This is why you hear so many people say that the church is full of hypocrites, I can't deny that, as there is a bit of a hypocrite in us all. Please receive this in love when I say that Christians are people, too, and make some really terrible decisions at times, thus the reason for Jesus Christ..

This brief chapter is to acknowledge my MCWC family that played a major part of the village, as the village remains a part of your life until the end of your life on this earth. That's what makes the village so incredibly valuable. There are far too many people to mention in this part of the village, but believe me, they know who they are, and I'll end this chapter by saying, "Love you, Metro."

Chapter Six

Coach

Often, you'll hear someone say that my coach was like a father figure to me. Though it seems like a noble gesture, and for many people that may be true, when you think about it, it's very sad.

I can remember how often I've referenced my high school basketball coach as a father figure. When I look back on it, a Monday through Friday dose of consistency over a six-to-seven-month time frame., consistently teaching, training, yelling, disciplining by running instead of spankings, and encouraging, while remaining stoic and strict at the same time; I believed this was everything I would've wanted and needed in a father to steer me in the right direction.

When it came to teaching, he would demonstrate what to do defensively using hard and intense motions. If I'm being honest, watching him demonstrate could be downright scary, and we all knew that we weren't going to do it that way, but we understood what it meant. We used to call my coach Chuck Norris because there was a real resemblance between the two. For those of you who may not know who Chuck Norris is, he was a martial artist who was a popular actor in the late 70s and 80s. There was a natural fear that I had of him because he never really smiled. I understood why he carried himself that way; so that his players would fear him and in turn be more likely to do exactly what he said to do.

The training was a brutal part of the yearly process, beating your body into physical submission. This is actually a biblical principle, as 1ˢᵗ Corinthians 9:27 says, *"But I discipline my body and keep it under control."* We had to run three miles a day in the heat during preseason workouts. This consisted of running around the local park, as one time around was supposed to be equivalent to one mile, but I have a feeling it may have been a little more than that. We would take off running from the starting point, the school parking lot. You could see the entire course around the park from that parking lot. There were a few blind spots, and one was near the public swimming pool, and believe me, nearly everyone would stop and walk in that spot. There were always a few that would run hard the entire time, and most of them had no chance of playing and were simply trying to impress Coach. Sometimes, closer to the end of preseason, he would get in his blue Chevy S-10 and drive around the park to ensure that no one was walking.

Once, during the preseason, they were holding cheerleading tryouts in the gym at the same time as our workouts. We were all showing off, trying to impress the girls, and I went running and jumping, trying to swing on the rim with two hands and slipped, landing with a *BOOM* face down on the floor. I used my hands to brace my fall, and being embarrassed popped right back up, while my other teammates were dying laughing.

Coach heard the laughing and knew we were out there playing around. He came out and said, "GET DOWN TO THE WEIGHT ROOM." At the time, I hadn't really felt any pain, just embarrassment, as I had to deal with the onslaught of jokes that were being thrown my way. I had to take it, because if that had been anybody else, I would've been doing the same thing. But as I went to pick up a dumbbell, a sharp pain went through my wrist and I dropped the weight. I looked down at my right wrist and noticed it was swollen. I went over and showed it to Coach, and I must say he was not happy.

"How the h@#^ did that happen?" I let him know that I had fallen in the gym and he told me that I needed to go see "Doc."

Doc was the name of the athletic trainer, and when I went to see him, he took one look and said, "you need to go to the emergency room, as it might be broken."

I walked to the clinic, and they told me that I needed to call my mom because they were going to need to have an x-ray, as they were quite certain it was broken. When I called my mom and told her that my wrist was probably broken, her response to me was, "Aww S#%#!" See, that response means another bill where I'm from. I hung up the phone, thinking to myself that I didn't try to get hurt. The x-ray confirmed a hairline fracture, and I was going to need a cast on for six weeks.

I was devastated, the season was about five weeks away, and in my mind, I wasn't missing it. I continued with preseason workouts, everything that I could do without my right hand. It was actually a blessing in disguise, as I began to use my left hand a lot more. It came rather easily to me, then I thought back to when somebody told me that my father was ambidextrous, and I knew that had something to do with it. Later on down the road, when my son was young, we determined that he was ambidextrous, and I can remember thinking about the link to my father once again.

We were about a week away from the season-opening tournament. My wrist was feeling fine, though still in a cast, and I was thinking how do I get this cast off without going back to the doctor? I walked over to my uncle BJ's and told him that I felt fine, but I really needed to get this cast taken off.

He looked at me and said, "Ah, boy, you better not tell your mom that I did this for you." He had me soak my cast in a bucket of water, and then he used a hacksaw and began to cut it. I was super scared that he was going to cut my arm off, and he looked at me, saying "Be still, boy, I ain't gonna hurt you."

About three minutes later, the cast was off, and I was free. Believe it or not, neither my mom nor my grandmother said a word, it was like they had forgotten that I had the cast on in the first place.

When I showed up at practice the next day without the cast, Coach knew something was up, saying, "I thought you said the cast was coming off in six weeks?" I didn't want to lie to him, so before I could say anything, he just walked away. It was like he knew and he didn't want me to lie to him either. In that moment, I felt like my father-figure had just given me the ok to play and that he was willing to look the other way. I knew then that I would run through a brick wall for that man.

You hear that phrase a lot in sports, your players running through a brick wall for their coaches. Every child wants to be led, guided, disciplined, and pointed in the right direction for their own good. That's what was happening to me. I remember how it felt when I frustrated or upset him, but I also remember how I felt when he gave me a hard high-five or a hard slap on the behind and said, "GOOD JOB, Q!!" It was like that was all I ever needed, wanted, or desired from a man; affirmation, acknowledgement, and more than either of those, a man to be proud of me.

Some of you may have grown up with a father who was a no-nonsense type of person and some of the funniest times was when they let their guard down. One moment comes to mind as it pertains to my coach, when we won a big game against a rival that had beaten us up for years. We were in the locker room celebrating, and Coach came in and slammed the door, *BOOM!* We all stopped and looked around, thinking he couldn't possibly be mad.

He said, "DA@#@$, FELLAS... where's the music? Turn the box on!"

We blasted that thing and "2 Legit 2 Quit" by MC Hammer came on, and for the first time ever, we saw coach, the touch guy, aka Chuck Norris, cut a rug (for you youngsters, that means dance). He was proud of us, so he came down to our level. He had been preaching on how to be tough for years.

When I think about it, every adult male who was ever an influence up until that point had always talked about being tough; men don't cry, don't be no punk, being soft will get you hurt, never let a man walk up on you, you make sure you bomb first. This mentality is embedded deep into the soul of a man and often comes out in the wrong way toward the people he loves the most, for me, that was my wife and children. However, there were many times of laughter and joy, just like my coach choosing to kick it with us, even if it was only for a minute or two. You experience another side of them. I know that my family saw and felt that too, they should've just felt it more than the former.

Though Coach was a father-figure to me, he may not have known it, but I'm sure he was as so many of us were suffering from the epidemic of fatherlessness. I don't ever remember him telling me that he loved me or anything, he didn't have to, because I was well aware that he wasn't my father, but he gave me exactly what I needed from a father during those high school years.

After the season, he would go down and teach and do drills with some of the elementary kids, and he asked if I'd help demonstrate for the kids. I would've done anything for him. It was cool to hear him introduce me to the kids and talk about my hoop attributes, I was soaking up. One time in particular, he asked me to demonstrate shooting a jump shot, and I missed six or seven shots in a row. He looked at me and said, "The object is to make them." He had half a grin, and I could do nothing but smile and started to make shots.

Though maybe everybody didn't feel the same way that I did, I was grateful for what he had been to and for me. If he gets a chance to read this book, I'd like to thank him. For many of us without a relationship with our biological fathers, we see this as love, and the thoughts in the mind of the fatherless is, "Man, I wish he could've been my dad." Shout out to Coach J.B.M.

Here's where the mindset of believing that my coach was a father-figure takes a turn. I took everything that I thought I needed as kid, that he provided, and began to parent that way. There wasn't a real blueprint for me, and so instead of fathering them, I began to coach them. I felt the need to carry myself with the same demeanor as my coach, wanted to be feared, respected, and a dictator (my way or the highway). None of those things are how a father should carry himself. My kids walked on eggshells, as we did in practice. Any teaching points were done with a scowl, as it was in practice. When it was time for discipline or correction, it was articulated by yelling and a mean mug. In my era of sports, this sort of behavior was common. My favorite collegiate coach, who I felt I would've loved to play for, was Bobby Knight of the University of Indiana. If you know who that is, then you will understand my style of parenting. Looking back, there was no excuse for it. Though I was coaching them, I was parenting out of anger toward my father. I always believed that I thrived best under tough love, so that's what I thought that my children needed as well. I couldn't have been more wrong. I pray that all my children will forgive me for the errors of my ways. I'm sure there were and maybe still are residual resentment, anger, bitterness, and maybe even the feeling of "F My Dad.".

Not every player could play under coach Bobby Knight, they saw his style as bullying, but if you ask some of the players who loved and revered him, they would probably tell you otherwise. Once I realized how wrong I was and how it had negatively affected my wife and children, it broke my heart. I can still see their faces, their tears, and the longing in their hearts to want to do their best for me, especially my son. Though I know he knows how much I love him, I was far too hard on him, even as a kid, because he was a such a good player. It started out fun, me teaching him the game, but the competitor in me as a player begin to take over as a father, who was parenting like an old school coach to a bunch of kids. Basketball became an idol because I wanted my son to be great; however, I truly believe that the way I carried myself ruined it for him. He ended up having shoulder problems during high school, which derailed his future in the sport, as he officially played in two varsity games over a four-year period., one during his freshman year and his final game during his senior year.

If you've ever seen the movie *Rudy*, my son was able to have one of those real-life moments. It was like God blessed him with one shining moment. In December of 2020, right in the middle of the COVID pandemic, my son's shoulder had dislocated again, and his basketball career was pretty much over. His coach was going to allow him to play in one game. It had been three years since I saw my son play. During this time, there weren't any spectators in the stands, but his Athletic Director, who was a really nice guy, allowed my wife and I to sit in our usual seats at the top of the bleachers. I got there early just to watch my son in warmups. It had been so long.

Finally, the time came for him to enter the game, and after a couple of trips down the floor, the ball was swung to him by his favorite assist man, Jack. He caught it in the corner and shot a three pointer, which hit nothing but net. The reaction of his teammates was so thundering loud, you would've thought the gym was full of fans. They had seen what he had gone through, and again, it was a real-life *Rudy* moment, except my son could play.

As my wife and I watched, the tears flowed down her face, while I did everything I could to hold them back. When I knew that basketball was over for my son, the Lord spoke to me and revealed that he had allowed these shoulder issues to plague my son so that he no longer had to put up with me. He let me know that he had given me time after time to change and I didn't do it. The moment that I heard that, I sobbed like a child, as he had revealed what my family had experienced and how I allowed my own anger and bitterness toward my father to rule over my life, showing me the negative impact it had on my wife and children.

If they ever read this book, I want to tell them that I am deeply sorry for it all, and I pray that they find a place in their hearts to forgive me. I pray that they receive understanding, not an excuse, for my actions. I only wanted to see them do great things, and I thought that the way my coach impacted me was the way I needed to do it.

Though I love and thank my coach for being a father figure, I never really knew him as the father he was for his own children. He had his own family, and I'm sure he wasn't the same way with them as he was with us a coach.

I truly believe that he cared about us players, as I can remember him making the bus take us to our homes because he knew we didn't have rides from the high school in the winter. When we would have early morning practices, he would drive to our neighborhoods and pick us up in his pickup truck, and we'd pile in the back and huddle up together. It was brutally cold, but it beat walking any day.

From now on, I see these men who hold roles of influence for young and many fatherless kids as men who provide some elements of a father, but they could never take the place of all that a child is supposed to learn from their father. The hope is for those who read this or maybe have fathered like this will understand that if your biological father has been missing or absent in your life, hopefully you were blessed to have an amazing step-father, but if not, only your Heavenly Father can fill that role, that void, and be listed as your genuine father figure in this life.

Chapter Seven

Who Am I?

I n order to properly set up this chapter, it's important to understand the phrase "Wrestling with God," which is a reference used in multiple places in the Bible. The story that I'd like to reference is that of the one in first book of the Bible, the book of Genesis. The title of this passage is "Jacob Wrestles with God." Genesis 32:22-30 says, *"The same night he arose and took his two wives, his two female servants, and his eleven children, and crossed the ford of the Jabbok. He took them and sent them across the stream, and everything else that he had. And Jacob was left alone. And a man wrestled with him until the breaking of the day. When the man saw that he did not prevail against Jacob, he touched his hip socket, and Jacob's hip was put out of joint as he wrestled with him. Then he said, "Let me go, for the day has broken." But Jacob said, "I will not let you go unless you bless me." And he said, "Jacob." Then he said, "Your name shall no longer be called Jacob, but Israel, for you have striven (struggle or fight) with God and with men, and have prevailed." Then Jacob asked him, "Please tell me your name." But he said, "Why is it that you ask my name?" And there he blessed him. So Jacob called the name of the place Peniel, saying , "For I have seen God face to face and yet my life has been delivered."*

When I was going through one of the darkest times of my life, a member of my church family came up to me and said, "You need to wrestle with God." I had no idea what that meant at the time. So, I did. I came to God and asked him to bless me and that I wasn't leaving until He did, so the fight began. I got tossed around like a rag doll, as He had been waiting for me to get to the point of being at the end of myself.

When you run out of options and realize that all your ways haven't worked, outside of God's roadmap, it's like an MMA fight when a fighter is being submitted and has to tap out. It felt as if the Lord had me in a hold, not one with an intent to hurt but one to control, hold, and calm a broken and outraged soul. He whispered to me and said that all I truly needed to do was to submit to Him wholeheartedly. Give up my pride, give up my arrogance, give up the cockiness, give up my plans, and submit to Him.

After a long period (years) of trying to fight, buck, and do whatever I could to get free from the hold that He had on me, I ran out of gas and had nothing left, so I chose to submit to Him.

This kind of submission requires a daily submission to anything and everything that comes my way, attempting to turn me back into everything that I've always been.

I'm grateful that He never let me go, as that's what father's do, we never let go. We hang on, no matter what our children may be facing, we hang onto them in love.

If you are a believer in Jesus Christ, you must believe that God has that same hold on your children and that He will keep them protected the same way He's kept and protected you.

I really thought I was a tough guy, but I was no match for the love of God. He held on tight when I attempted to fight and buck as he was trying to reach the little boy who longed for his earthly father and was still longing.

After that, things began to change. I was seeing my heart beginning to weaken, soften, and was tired of fighting it. It felt like a scene from a movie, like *The Exorcist*, there was evil inside, and my Father in heaven had to cast it out. And it fought, this wasn't a quick fight, it lasted for years, some days it just may spark up again. I had to reach the point where my flesh, my alter ego, and the dark side of me were tired of fighting.

The thought that I have today is that the other side of me isn't dead, but I must kill him a little more each day that I'm blessed to have on this earth. My father choosing not to be in my life is not an excuse to treat people in a negative way, especially the ones who love me the most. Many of us who struggle with being fatherless tend to hold this over those we hurt as the excuse of all excuses to hurt someone. Well, it's not. If you are still alive, God has provided you with grace and mercy to be here whether your father has been in your life or not. Why? Because your heavenly father has always been there. Remember, He knew you before you were formed in your mother's womb. The key is understanding that while wrestling with God, His heart never gets angry, as it remains all love.

Are you ready to wrestle with God?

"Who am I?" That is a question that most people stand in a mirror and ask themselves. To be honest, most of us walk through life without ever really getting a clear answer. The average reason for that is always based on the source. Meaning, who do you think should be able to give you that answer? Your parents, grandparents, other family members, friends, teachers, coaches, bosses, co-workers, yourself? What is the source? Notice that I didn't mention God. If we knew He was our source, there would really be no need for this question or this chapter, but this question seems to stump so many of us, typically until we are much older in age.

There are so many answers that I've had over the years as it pertained to "Who Am

I?" A man, a husband, a father, a son, a grandson, a brother, a cousin, a friend. Those are all true, but those are all the things that are obvious about all of us. But is that who I am? If I'm being honest about the old me that fights to stay alive, he's funny, confident, cocky, arrogant, angry, fearful, loyal, family, leader, baller, coach, jealous, envious, protective, guarded, dark-hearted, misunderstood, selfish, greedy (lover of money), entrepreneur, grinder, survivor, fighter, lover of music, perplexed, complex, enraged, lost, found, a deflector, a defender, a conditional lover, bright, creative, sincere, and complicated. I'm sure there are more that I haven't listed, maybe some I am unaware of and some I'm too ashamed to list, but the hard part about walking with God is how to kill off all the things that I mentioned that aren't like Him at all.

Your parents are supposed to be the direct link, not to tell who you are but to nurture you into who your Heavenly Father has created you to be. This sounds rather simple, right? The problem with that is that so many of us weren't under the provision of that kind of household. Maybe your mother wasn't there, maybe your father wasn't there, maybe neither of them were there, still, yet, you are breathing and able to read what I'm writing. That's the proof that your Heavenly Father was there all along. The question that most of us may ask in response to that is, "Where has my Heavenly Father been, as my life has been nothing but trauma after trauma?" This is the basis or what I like to call the trunk of our tree of identity. You were not supposed to raise yourself; you were not supposed to teach yourself; you were not supposed to love yourself, and when you really think about it, you didn't. The reason that you are still here today is because your Heavenly Father has always been there. There were people He sent into your life who showed you love, showed you how to read, how to talk, how to walk, how to tie your shoes, and so much more. The problem is that trauma can often wipe out those memories and cause us to focus on all the pain and heartache that we have endured.

There will always be a battle that we will face with sin, also known as wrongdoing, wickedness, immoral things, and evil. The word sin sounds so religious and heinous, well that's because it is. However, I would challenge you to look at sin as simply most of our horrible decisions in life. Many people may say, "Well, I didn't abuse myself." That is true, but it was a horrible decision by your abuser who chose to abuse you. If we know their history, then we probably know of the horrible decisions that were acted out upon them, and it just might shed a sense of understanding as to why they were the way they were and why the consequences of our horrible decisions will always impact someone else and quite possibly cause them to make their own horrible decisions. These consequences are often passed down from generation to generation. That understanding does not excuse their actions, but it does allow them to be seen as flawed individuals. Oftentimes, this will make forgiving them a tad bit easier. The combination of those horrible decisions will often lead to major reasons for your issues as it pertains to your identity., leaving you to constantly ask the question, "Who Am I?"

When you didn't have the proper connection or the proper protocol as it pertains to your parents and their relationship with their Heavenly Father, issues within your identity are basically inevitable. Now, remember, our identity issues are the trunk of the tree, which lead to branches and leaves that so many of us are familiar with and that we walk in every single day. "An estimated 31.1% of U.S. adults experience some sort of anxiety disorder at some time in their lives."[13] If you're anything like me, you've struggled with anger and rage at some point in your life.

"Nearly, 7.8% of people in the U.S. have intense, poorly controlled, or inappropriate levels of anger."[14] Maybe you battle depression, well, you're not alone as, "Approximately 9.5% of American adults will suffer from a depressive illness each year."[15] There are so many more items linked to our identity issues, the trunk of the tree, that I could discuss, but the reality is that it all has a direct connection, for many of us, to the root of the tree, which is fatherlessness.

The key that I've found is to somehow, some way, grasp a glimpse of how your Heavenly Father sees you, as His view of you

---

[13] www.nimh.nih.gov

[14] strivemental.com

[15] www.hopkinsmedicine.org

is the only one that matters, and this will shatter the identity issues in your life or the "Who Am I" that has long been a question that you've asked yourself deep within your soul.

For me, my Heavenly Father reminded me that He had always been there. From the time I was born onto the earth to the time that I'll leave it, He's going to be there.

All of us have a desire for our fathers to tell us who we are and to reaffirm the fact that they absolutely love us unconditionally. When I think of how my Heavenly Father sees and talks about me, He says, "That's my son, Q.O., and I'm super proud of him. Yes, he has a lot of flaws, but I know that he loves his Daddy, Me. I love his willingness to try and to keep striving ahead. Yes, often I must send angels around him because he can be a little hotheaded at times, and sometimes I may allow him to reap those hurtful consequences of his actions. Still, I love him, and I will never leave him, never!" That's how I hear it, because that's what I believe a father would say, if nothing else, "I love my child unconditionally."

The truth about how He sees us is already written. Whether or not we know Him closely will determine how we experience His love, walk in His love, and receive our identity from the one who created us, all of us. Yes, He's that big!!

I challenge you to get to know Him so that he can affirm your identity and answer the question of "Who you are" once and for all. Take a look at the trees below to see the example of a tree with Him and a tree without Him and decide which one looks familiar to you:

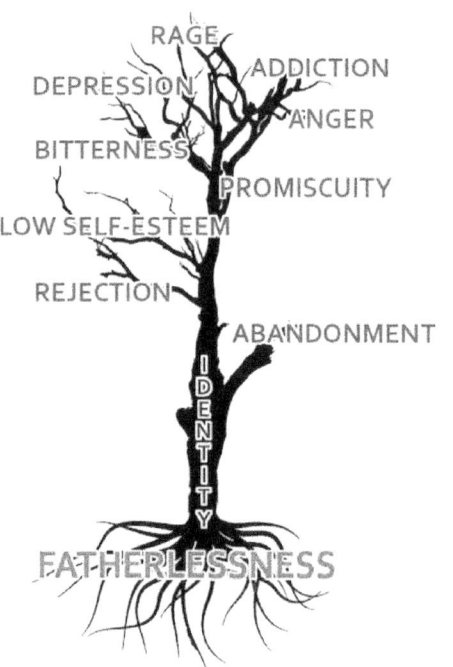

LOVING FISHERMAN
CONFIDENT PRAYERFUL
PATIENCE SUCCESSFUL
SERVANT TRUSTWORTHY
BOLD GIVING
CHRISTIAN

HEAVENLY FATHER
(WORD)

Chapter Eight

What's Your Name Again?

One Sunday evening in September 2019, I received a call from my mother, and she told me that my aunt on my father's side was sick. This was the same aunt I mentioned earlier, who was the only one from that family who treated me like family. I realized that I hadn't talked to her in years and asked my mom if she could find her phone number. A few minutes later she called back with her number. I immediately reached out and gave her a call. When she answered, I smiled, as I hadn't heard her voice in such a long time.

I said, "Hey, how are you doing?"

She replied, "Pretty good, who is this?"

"It's one of your oldest nephews," and she screamed out my name.

It was a surreal feeling, that feeling when you know that somebody truly loves you.

We talked for about half an hour, and she told me about all her health problems. I felt horrible that I hadn't reached out to her in such a long time. I could tell that talking for long periods of time was difficult for her, but I could also tell that she didn't want the call to end. As the call began to wind down, I thanked her for always treating me like family and that I loved her for it.

In her one-of-a-kind voice, she said, "I love you, too, nephew."

I let her know that I would be in town in December and that I would come by and visit her. She was excited to hear that and said that she couldn't wait to meet my children. We said "I love you" to one another again and hung up.

About a month later, I received a call that she had passed away.

I thanked the Lord for allowing me to have one last conversation with her in order to tell her how much I loved and appreciated her.

Don't take time for granted, if you have a loved one you haven't talked to in a while, believe me when I tell you, they would love to hear from you.

Once I received the information about her funeral services, I wasn't sure if I would attend, but I knew in my heart that I owed it to her to pay my respects. There was a weird, eerie feeling deep in my soul, as the only thing that I could think about was the fact that I hadn't seen my father in twenty-nine years. During the week before my aunt's funeral, I was uneasy. I went back and forth about whether I should attend the funeral or not. Each time I thought that I shouldn't go, I just kept thinking about my aunt and how, from that side of my family, she was the only one who ever treated me like family. It wasn't about me or my father, it was about me paying respect to my aunt.

The day came, Saturday morning, and my wife and I had about an hour and a half drive in order to get to the location of the funeral. We arrived only minutes prior to the start of the funeral. When we walked in the door, I ran into a few people I knew from my hometown and let the nervousness begin.

We sat in the very last row, and sitting right in front of me was a guy whose grandmother lived across the street from my grandmother and he would be there from time to time as kids and we would play together, we called him "Saint." My mother had told me that every time she would run into him, he would always ask about me. I tapped him on his shoulder, he turned around and did a double take, put out his hand, and as I went to dap him up (shake hands), he grabbed my hand and just held it. I felt the love instantly. I don't think that was a coincidence, as I needed to feel loved in that place.

As my father's family entered the room, there was the feeling of rejection and abandonment starting to rear its ugly head. My wife grabbed my hand and said, "Are you okay?"

Though I wasn't, I tried to play it tough and said, "Aw, yeah, I'm cool."

The truth was that I was a mess inside. And then I saw him, my father, a man I hadn't seen for twenty-nine years.

We were asked to read the obituary silently, and as I read it, they listed all her nieces and nephews, yet my name was not there. Those two feelings, rejection and abandonment, were ramping up higher and higher. Then I saw that all her nephews were pallbearers, and I was really hurting.

The service began to roll along, and then my father got up to speak about his sister. It was the first time that my wife had seen my father in our eighteen-year marriage. As I watched him speak, I realized that I knew nothing about the man. I sat there and thought, do I really look like him, talk like him, act like him? I was that little boy all over again, looking at his photos in my mother's yearbook.

As we came to the end of the service and it was time to view the body, my brother, my father's son, who I had met a few years prior, was sitting in the front row as a pallbearer. Once I crossed his path, he hopped up smiling and gave me the biggest hug. I could tell in his eyes that he was hoping this was going to be an opportunity for my father and I to reconnect, but I had my doubts.

Once the funeral came to an end and people began to mingle and talk to old friends and family, I saw so many people I knew and hadn't seen in decades. After about fifteen or twenty minutes of catching up with old family and friends, I decided to simply slide out the back door. As I walked toward the door, I heard the Lord clearly say to me, "If you walk out that door, you will regret it for the rest of your life."

I stopped and told my wife, "I have to go speak to my father."

She looked at me, surprised, and asked, "What are you going to say?"

I replied, "I have no idea, but I need to say something."

There was a line of about five or six people who were shaking hands with my father. So, I got into the line, and as I got closer and closer, I looked up, and my brother had made his way right beside my father and was all smiles. The closer I got, the more I trembled inside, and when there were only a couple of people in front of me, the trembling became almost overwhelming, I thought maybe I was having some kind of panic attack, and in that moment, I felt a hand in the middle of my back, but when I turned around, there was no one there.

Then I heard the Lord say in a calm way, "Don't worry, I've got you. You don't have to be afraid, I'm here."

Once I reached my father and stood before him, he stuck out his hand and began to shake it and said, "Now, what's your name again?" He didn't even know who I was, and so I leaned in and spoke directly in his ear, saying only my name. When I pulled back, he looked as if he had seen a ghost. He began to look around as if his cover was blown, and my brother's smile slowly went away, the expression on his face turning to confusion.

I leaned back in and said, "Don't worry about it, man. I'm good. I'm really good." As soon as I said that, every chain, shackle, and weight that had been on me fell off, and that weight I had been carrying for all my life no longer existed. I stood before that man and thought to myself that I was bigger than him in every way, physically, mentally, emotionally, spiritually, and that it was his loss for not being in my life.

In that very moment, the Lord spoke to me and said, "All this time, you didn't think he wanted you, when the truth of the matter is, I kept you from him, as you belong to me."

For the first time in my life, I knew who I was and whose I was, I was the son of my Heavenly Father, and He had always been there for me, even when I lived opposite of His will and His ways. That's what fathers do, and that's how much He loved me and continues to love me.

Once I walked away from my father, I turned and saw my mother talking to my father's brother, my uncle, and she said, with his back turned to me, "This is my son."

He turned around, and when he saw me, something happened that had never happened to me before, he just stood there, staring at me, and after about seven seconds, he stuck out his hand and said, "Nice to meet you, man." That was my first time meeting the man, but his response to meeting me said it all. The moment was so surreal that I almost forgot that I was at a funeral.

I sought out my cousin, my aunt's daughter, and she was in tears. I approached her and she turned, looked at me, and just hugged me. She said, "You came."

I replied, "I had to come to pay my respects to your mother, as she was the only one..."

She went on to finish my sentence, "Who treated you like family." She went onto say, "You know, she called me right after she talked to you a few weeks ago. She really did love you."

I looked into her eyes and said, "I know she did, and I loved her, and that's why I'm here."

As my wife and I exited and headed back home, we got onto the highway, and she simply looked at me and said, "What are you feeling?"

I responded with one word. "Freedom."

Chapter Nine

Freedom

So much time had been spent in anger, rage, pain, and internal agony over never having a relationship with my father, but for the first time ever, that was no longer there. I have to admit that there was an overwhelming sadness as I entered this place of freedom. It wasn't sadness for me but for so many others who have been struggling with the same epidemic of fatherlessness.

When I got back into town from my aunt's funeral, I called one of my boys, MH, and told him what happened. His response was, "Man, that is just crazy!" I could hear the anger and frustration in his voice, but I was free from it, finally.

Freedom doesn't mean that thoughts or memories don't cross my mind, it just means that my response is completely different. I actually felt sad for my father. I thought about what kind of turmoil, mentally, emotionally, and spiritually, he's had to carry and still carries. The toll it must take to harbor a lie amongst those who are in his life who have believed he only has two sons when he has three. Seeing me in public with a room full of people who knew him personally, the amount of fear that must've overcome him, knowing that his biggest lie could be uncovered. What a really sad way to live, but I could only feel that while walking in freedom because I had walked in my own lies and tried my best to keep them hidden. Most of us reference those things as skeletons in the closet. If we're being honest, some of us have cemeteries and not just a couple of skeletons. Me, personally, I like to use the analogy of having bodies buried under the house and you have to do any and everything to keep the smell from getting out, causing others to suspect something foul is going on. We all have them, places we don't like for our minds to go, we'd rather keep it covered, but in this instance with my father, I am alive and well, and now he has to live with the fact that he chose the lie over his son when he had the opportunity to make it right. Darkness continues to win and reign over his life, whether he accepts it or lives like it does or not.

In John 8:31-32, Jesus said *"If you abide in my word, you are truly my disciples, and you will know the truth, and the truth will set you free."*[16]

I thank God for setting me free when He exposed the truth to me about being my Father and always being there for me and that

---

[16] Unless otherwise noted, all biblical passages referenced are in the ESV Student Study Bible, Crossway Books (2011).

He kept me from my earthly father. The final meaning for the "F" word on the front of this book is "Freedom," "Free From My Dad!"

I do pray that my father receives freedom before his days on this earth come to an end and he chooses to die with his foolish and selfish pride. The choice is all his own, as God gives us all the free will to choose how we live and whom we choose to serve, and there are dire consequences for those choices that don't align with His ways.

Walking in freedom isn't always easy, but having real clarity is bliss. Understanding who I am and whose I am are the real answers to a pain and darkness so deep no earthly person could ever cure it, not my wife, my children, my mama, my grandma, or anyone in my village. Those answers can truly only come from the one who created me, and only when walking in freedom will those answers begin to make sense. It is there and only there where new life begins and you have the ability to leave the chains, shackles, and heavy baggage behind once and for all.

I have the freedom to embrace my whole truth, while gaining the understanding that none of the negative defines who I am in the eyes of my Heavenly Father. He sees me differently, He sees me like a father is supposed to see his child, with love.

While walking in freedom and receiving clarity, I knew exactly what I had been slotted to do; tell my story to anyone who would listen, as the epidemic of fatherlessness was bigger than I could ever imagine. I needed to be a light to those stuck in this darkness and let them know that it's his loss and not theirs and to no longer give him that power, as he doesn't deserve it at all. If they will hear that, then maybe they will desire to get to know their Heavenly Father if they don't already, and if they do, maybe they will see Him differently than ever before.

It is important to understand the dynamic of this epidemic. It tends to be the cause of a lot of the dysfunction families face as it pertains to raising children. See for yourself.

According to thefatherlessgeneration.wordpress.com:

- 63% of youth suicides are from fatherless homes (US Dept. Of Health/Census) - 5 times the average.

- 90% of all homeless and runaway children are from fatherless homes – 32 times the average.

- 85% of all children who show behavior disorders come from fatherless homes – 20 times the average. (Center of Disease Control)

- 80% of rapists with anger problems come from fatherless homes – 14 times the average. (Justice & Behavior, Vol 14, p. 403-26)

- 71% of all high school dropouts come from fatherless homes – 9 times the average. (National Principals Association Report)

- 70% of youths in state-operated institutions come from fatherless homes – 9 times the average. (U.S. Dept. Of Justice, Sept. 1988)

- 85% of all youths in prison come from fatherless homes – 20 times the average. (Fulton

Co. Georgia, Texas Dept. of Correction)

- A 2002 Department of Justice survey of 7,000 inmates revealed that 39% of jail inmates lived in mother-only households. Approximately 46% of jail inmates in 2002 had a previously incarcerated family member. One-fifth experienced a father in prison or jail.

- Daughters of single parents without a father involved are 53% more likely to marry as teenagers, 711% more likely to have children as teenagers.

- About 40% of children in father-absent homes have not seen their father at all during the past year.

- 26% of absent fathers live in a different state than their children.

- 50% of children living absent of their father have never set foot in their father's home.

- 24 million children (34%) live absent their biological father.

These numbers are staggering and downright sad to see. The one statistic that stands out is that there are twenty-four million children living without their biological father. Let me paint a picture for you. If you add the total population of New York City, Los Angeles, Chicago, Houston, Phoenix, Philadelphia, San Antonio, San Diego and Dallas, you would still be a bit short of the total number of children that are absent of their biological fathers.[17] This is the reason for

---

[17] worldpopulationreview.com

calling the issue of fatherlessness an epidemic. The next time you are in the mall, a movie theater, a concert, or the grocery store, stop and look around and realize that probably half of the people there are or have dealt with some form of fatherlessness, and we wonder why the culture is dealing with so many mental, emotional, spiritual, and even physical issues, where many will stem from issues with identity.

It's time to look at the root of the problems below.

Below, you will see a tree with the root of fatherlessness and one where the Heavenly Father is the root, where you will see a completely different set of branches:

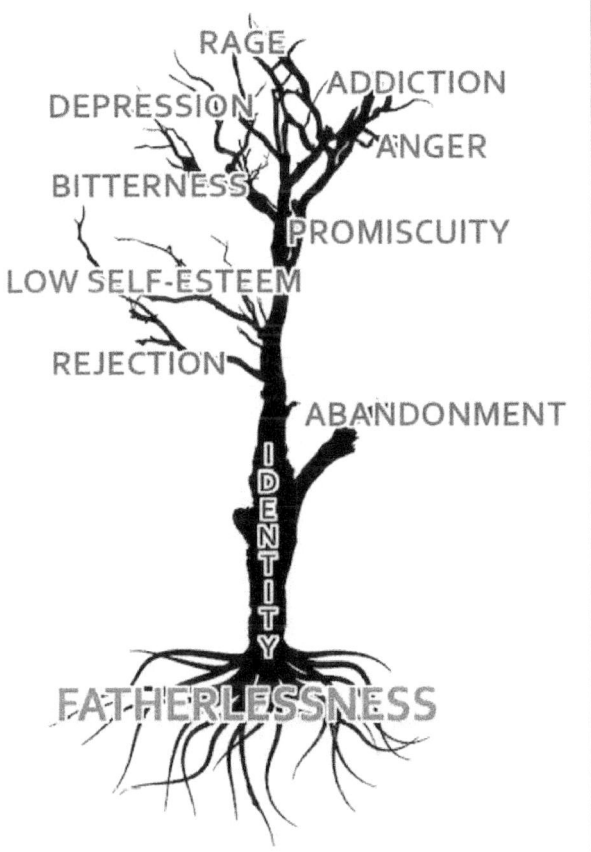

Even if you couldn't see it and you heard the items from each tree, ask yourself, which one would you choose? Now, think about someone you know who may be a product of the fatherless tree and see if they may seem to be struggling from any of the problems listed. If you, the reader, are a product of fatherlessness, do any of those items look or sound familiar to you?

The role of a father is so powerful that their absence has plagued mankind for generations past and will for generations to come unless we begin to reach fathers and encourage them to play the role that God intended, as well as introducing the fatherless to their Heavenly Father, and break this viscous cycle for future generations.

When I think about so many people I know and where they are today who grew up without their fathers, it's easy to see many of the items that have plagued their hearts from the fatherless tree. If they are anything like me, the road has been long and the pain has been real. However, for most men, the majority will deny it's effect, but if you look deep into their lives, I truly believe that you'll find the fatherless child is very much alive on the inside of them.

Once I understood that God has been my father from before I was created in my mother's womb, I knew whose boy I was and how proud my father was of me. It changed my life. My identity was finally defined and cemented.

I believe that most of us struggle with some form of identity issue. For me, the question was who am I really? Am I what people think I am or am I what I wish I could be like, or am I really a person full of fear? Fear of abandonment, fear of rejection, fear of being alone, fear of being found out that much of who I was acting out to be was simply a cover up of who I really was. I had a way to make people laugh, so often that would come at the cost of other people. Being a bully, only because I was afraid of being bullied. Underneath it all, I had a heart and wanted the best for people, but during my adolescence, teens, and twenties, I just lived in so much fear that I could never really let it be known. I'm sure there are a few people in my life who could attest to being with me when that guard was let down, and more than likely, they saw a different person. Someone most people didn't see and wouldn't believe if they were to ever tell me what they had encountered at certain moments. Someone who was softer, serious, driven for something deeper in this life, and for a few, a longing for a relationship with God.

Though I gave my life to Christ at the age of twenty-four, I was far from delivered from identity issues. I struggled with it as a husband, as a father, as a man claiming to be walking with God, but my heart was still questioning, "Who are you, really?" It would take twenty-one years before that answer would finally come.

God Bless my wife and children, as they took the brunt of a man who was struggling badly with who he was that he could only be what he thought he was supposed to be, or better yet, what he had been for the majority of his life; a fraud. A man who could only occasionally show that he had a soft side. Most of the time, he was hard and narcissistic, something he felt that he had to be for the majority of his life.

My identity issues, nor anyone else who is battling with identity issues, are an excuse to be a terrible, nasty person. Those are just major symptoms dwelling from the root problem of fatherlessness. The day that the chains were broken was the first time I heard from my Heavenly Father in a way that I knew it was him and was affirming in the way I had always desired from my biological father. As I mentioned, what I heard from the Lord, "You always thought he didn't want you, but the truth of the matter is, I kept you from him because you belong to me." That was a moment that I was free to be just like the father that I knew, the one who had been with me the entire time.

This transformation didn't happen overnight, as I had to go a few more years with the struggle because it was all I knew, until I was tired of running and I saw a crossroad. My Heavenly Father told me that I had to choose—walk with Him or don't, but if I chose the opposite of Him, He was going to allow me to go through some things that could be avoided if I chose Him. Well, I was a lot older and a bit wiser, and so I chose God once and for all. Ten toes down and only being concerned with how He sees me. Now, I wish to do everything that I can in my power to not let my dad down, my real dad, that is.

For the first time in my life, I'm settling into who I really am and have to spend each day fighting all those imitators that I had tried to be for so long and learn how to be good with who my Father called me to be. I have settled with the fact that I've been chosen. I don't say that in a prideful way but a humble way, because to know that out of many who were called, I was one who was chosen by my Father, with all of my dirt, followed by guilt, shame, and condemnation, He still loved me and wanted the best for me, if only I would truly submit my life to Him. When you think about it, that's what good and loving fathers do.

In Matthew 22:14, Jesus said, *"For many are called, but few are chosen"*[18].

---

[18] Unless otherwise noted, all biblical passages referenced are in the ESV Student Study Bible, Crossway Books (2011).

If you suffer from trauma that comes from the root of fatherlessness and you're reading this book, I think your Heavenly Father has chosen you. listen closely, and I'm certain you will hear him calling you.

From there, I was able to gain clarity of what my purpose was on this earth and how it was directly linked to the great commission.

In Matthew 28:19-20, Jesus said, *"Go therefore and make disciples of all nations, baptizing them in the name of the Father and of the Son and of the Holy Spirit, teaching them to observe all that I have commanded you. And behold, I am with you always, to the end of the age"*[19].

I often like to cross-reference scripture with different versions in order to gain further understanding and clarity but to also provide those who may not be familiar with the faith or

---

[19] Unless otherwise noted, all biblical passages referenced are in the ESV Student Study Bible, Crossway Books (2011).

reading the Bible a chance to gain an understanding of the purpose Jesus had for all Christians. Here's how the same passage of scripture reads from the Message Version of the Bible, *"Go out and train everyone you meet, far and near, in this way of life, marking them by baptism in the threefold name: Father, Son, and Holy Spirit. Then instruct them in the practice of all I have commanded you. I'll be with you as you do this, day after day after day, right up to the end of the age"*[20].

Going back to school and gaining a Master of Divinity allowed me to get the training needed to connect my fatherless story with my Heavenly Father's story and put them together to provide a blueprint for the millions who were just like me and how their success was directly connected to their identity and their purpose. This blueprint allowed me to

---

[20] Eugene H. Peterson and Mark A. Tabb, *The Message Remix*. Colorado Springs: Alive Communications, Inc, 2003.

easily throw out the invitation to introduce them to my Heavenly Father, who was also their Heavenly Father, thus that makes us siblings in Christ. Knowing that seems to put a crack in the wall that often surrounds a broken heart due to the absence of their father.

Back in the earlier chapters I talked about how my uncle would take us fishing. If you've ever been around people who fish, you'll certainly run into someone who has made their own bait. Now, nine times out of ten, it would stink to high heaven, but let them tell it, the fish couldn't help but to bite. That's how I would describe myself as it relates to purpose. I'm simply the bait. I've done so much dirt in my life that I can be looked at as stinky, grimy, slimy, dirty, filthy, nasty, bait. But for some reason, when casted out, the fish (people) are always attracted to it and desire a bite. Now, that's not putting me on some kind of pedestal, I'm simply explaining my purpose, also viewed as the calling.; to be some funky bait, still attractive enough for those looking for another way to be interested and willing to listen.

My Heavenly Father knew what I would go through, what I would face, the wrong that I would do, but just like the earthly father is supposed to, and many of them do, He stayed with me. He continued to groom me, mold me, shape me, until a time such as this.

To think that I would be writing a book is pretty laughable, just ask my beautiful wife.

Though this is my story, I'm sure that if you grew up without a relationship with your biological father, there are many things that sound similar, maybe close to identical, but trust me when I tell you that my Heavenly Father has your purpose all lined out, and if you're unsure about it, I suggest you seek Him out and give Him your life.

The thing about accepting the gift of salvation and becoming born again is that's the easy part. If you are reading this and there's a tugging on your heart where you know that you need to do this, but… let me guess, all the things that you don't believe you can do or aren't willing to do or let go of is hindering you making that decision, let me reassure you; that feeling resides in us all.

The way you have to view it is as an opportunity to get free from the worldly cycle of life that ultimately leads to despair and turmoil, and if you didn't or don't have a relationship with your biological father, then you need to go back and look at the tree with the root of fatherlessness and ask yourself if any of the branches listed there are prevalent in your life. If they are, this book is the bait, will you take it and let your Heavenly Father reel you in and clean you up? It's there and only there where you will find the peace and love that you have been looking for most of your life. Believe me, there is where your purpose lies, in Him, your Father. Let Him guide you, and you'll find that success is imminent.

The final piece is success, but it all depends on how success is being defined. I was what you would call one who has a "driver's" financial mentality, where having money equals success. I used to hear people say that money isn't everything, but I always replied, let me get some first and then I'll let you know. However, my Heavenly Father provided me with clarity as it pertains to my money driven mindset of success.

1st Timothy 6:10 says, *"For the love of money is a root of all kinds of evils. It is through this craving that some have wandered away from the faith and pierced themselves with many pangs"*[21]. Here's another scripture that I'd like to cross-reference with the Message Version, it says,

---

[21] Ibid.

"Lust for money brings trouble and nothing but trouble. Going down that path, some lose their footing in the faith completely and live to regret it bitterly ever after"[22]. Notice that it doesn't just say money is the root of all evil, it says the love or lust for it.

If you're being honest, there is some point and time that you had or maybe still have a love or lust for money. I can't lie, it's something that I still struggle with to this day. However, my Heavenly Father has reassured me that if I put all my efforts into loving Him, searching for Him, desiring Him and His will and His ways, making Him the top of my personal hierarchy, everything I'm looking for He's more than willing to give to me.

---

[22] Eugene H. Peterson and Mark A. Tabb, *The Message Remix*. Colorado Springs: Alive Communications, Inc, 2003.

For Psalms 37:4 says, *"Delight yourself in the Lord, and he will give you the desires of your heart"*[23].

I've often delighted myself in having money and have even had the audacity to blame God when I didn't have it (facepalm). God is not our personal genie, He doesn't work like that, He's a Father, the Ultimate Father. How many times did your parents tell you no or you're going to have to work for it? The only work that your Heavenly Father desires for you to do is to come after Him with everything in you.

Another passage of scripture I'll throw out there as it pertains to this is Matthew 6:33, where Jesus said, *"But seek first the kingdom of God*

---

[23] Unless otherwise noted, all biblical passages referenced are in the ESV Student Study Bible, Crossway Books (2011).

and his righteousness, and all these things will be added unto you"[24].

The problem is that we seek us first. Our lives, the wants and needs of my family, and we'll typically turn to God when we run into some kind of trouble. Sound familiar? That's how many of us are with our own earthly parents. Well, that's a whole other book, hopefully coming soon.

Wallowing in the abyss of identity issues for as long as I did, I was always seeking that place to fit in, be something and somebody. It's hard to do that when you really don't know who you are. My mother was great, my grandmother was amazing, and my stepfather was cool, but none of them were my dad. I couldn't erase or change the role in which God had ordained for earthly fathers, and because my father was absent, I was never affirmed by the one who had been slotted for

---

[24] Ibid.

that position, and thus I spent most of my life wandering and searching for what could fill that void. Through my long life of sinful nature, nothing ever came close. I thought that money, fame, and fortune would equal success, but I couldn't have been more wrong. Real success lies in the plan that your Heavenly Father has for you.

Remember way back when I mentioned that your Heavenly Father knew you before you formed in your mother's womb? He also knew why He was creating you, what He was putting you on this earth to accomplish for Him.

I'm certain that not everyone will agree with my definition of success, but when you've been searching for it for as long as I've searched, you realize that if you aren't in your purpose, then you are simply walking around in a fog until this short life comes to an end. Don't be like me and waste time giving power to a man that had no desire to have a relationship with me and how I let it delay what my Heavenly Father wanted me to do all along. Which is to show me who my real Father is and that He's been with me through all the ups and downs in my life, and his love is everlasting and will never die.

He desperately wants a relationship with you, and if you'd like I can lead you to him. If you've gotten to this point of the book, I truly believe that He's been knocking at your heart.

My Pastor of over twenty years used to always use this passage of scripture as it pertains to the knocking at your heart, Revelation 3:20 reads, *"Behold, I stand at the door and knock. If anyone hears my voice and opens the door, I will come into him and eat with him, and he with me"*[25].

---

[25] Ibid.

This is your Father reaching out to you, and He wants you to know Him, and He longs to affirm you, listen to you, guide you. He wants to free you from the chains of rejection and abandonment, show you who you really are to Him. Most of all, He sent his only son to die for you just so that He could love on you the way a father is supposed to love on his child, He's simply waiting for you to open the door.

If you want to open the door and take the first step of meeting the Father you have been longing for while dealing with the root of fatherlessness, simply turn the page. If you're not quite there, close the book and know that He'll be here, but understand that the clock is ticking, and you don't have to waste another moment without your "Dad." Your freedom is only one page away.

YOU DID IT!!!

Now, take a deep breath and read the following out loud.

> *"Hey, Dad, I've spent a lot of time longing for a loving relationship with my biological father, but now I realize that you, my Heavenly Father, have been there all along. This is new to me, but I'm certain that I want to get to know you, and even more than that, I need you to hold and love me as your child. I've messed up so many times in my life, so I guess that makes me a sinner. I truly believe that you sent your son Jesus Christ to die for my sins, and I also believe that on the third day, he rose from the dead and the tomb where his body laid is now empty. I've missed you, Dad, and now I can't wait to grow a relationship with you..."*

Just sit right there quietly, and I believe with everything in me He's going to meet you right where you are. Be patient, and if you feel something in this moment, that's Him, and that's what freedom feels like.